'Captivating, heartwarming and inspiring. The
and music open a window to a richer encounte
Song is nourishment for the weary, tender, searching soul.
Jo Walker, cofounder of STEER Education

'What a gift! Here is food for the heart, soul, mind and faithful living as Micah and Clare let the psalms sing afresh through their artwork and reflections. This is as beautiful as it is profound, and I commend it to you for your own devotions and as a rich source of resources to share with others.'
Mark Tanner, bishop of Chester

'Micah and Clare have created a beautiful, multisensorial entry point into the psalms. In this lovely book they give us an accessible way into these ancient songs, inviting connection with the created world, with our deepest human longings, with our everyday, often prosaic lives and with the one who loves us. Dwell, ponder, enjoy!'
Olivia Graham, bishop of Reading

'*Garden Song* is a delightful collaboration, with its delicate, evocative paintings and carefully observed reflections on human and divine nature, structured around psalms of worship, grief and joy. This is a collection to dip into at key moments, allowing the artist and author to help us notice God at work around us.'
The Rt Revd Dr Joanne Woolway Grenfell, bishop of Stepney

'The psalms are an unparalleled treasury for worship and prayer. They run the gamut of human emotion: life in its entirety brought into God's presence. In this book, Clare and Micah Hayns reflect with honesty and beauty in word and image, inspiring and challenging us to engage afresh with these ancient words. This is a resource which will enrich prayer and take us deeper into the heart of God.'
The Revd Canon Peter Moger, subdean, Christ Church, Oxford

'Micah's refreshing artwork complements perceptive reflections from Clare. A treasure of a book to savour and to share.'
Margaret Whipp, writer and spiritual director

'The Hebrew psalms have been a unique seed of human creativity. No other collection of poetry in the world has drawn out such a range and depth of imaginative response, and it is good to welcome this new contribution to that long history.'
Roger Wagner, artist and poet

'Clare and Micah have created a symphony for the heart with this powerful book… every part of me was engaged as I journeyed through Clare's beautifully vulnerable and edifying reflections, meditated on Micah's illustrations, soaked in the music and committed to God the prayers provided, written by heroes of the faith. I would advise anyone reading this book to savour it… you will meet God there. Wonderful!'
Lola Chapman, director of global advancement, One Collective

GARDEN SONG

BRF Ministries

15 The Chambers, Vineyard
Abingdon OX14 3FE
brf.org.uk | +44 (0)1865 319700

Bible Reading Fellowship (BRF) is a charity (233280) and company limited by
guarantee (301324), registered in England and Wales

ISBN 978 1 80039 237 3
First published 2024
10 9 8 7 6 5 4 3 2 1 0
All rights reserved

Text © Clare Hayns 2024
Illustrations © Micah Hayns 2024
This edition © Bible Reading Fellowship 2024
Cover image © Micah Hayns

The author asserts the moral right to be identified as the author of this work

Acknowledgements
Unless otherwise acknowledged, scripture quotations are taken from The New Revised Standard Version, Updated
Edition. Copyright © 2021 National Council of Churches of Christ in the United States of America. Used by permission.
All rights reserved worldwide.

Scripture quotations marked NIV are taken from The Holy Bible, New International Version (Anglicised edition) copyright
© 1979, 1984, 2011 by Biblica. Used by permission of Hodder & Stoughton Publishers, a Hachette UK company. All rights
reserved. 'NIV' is a registered trademark of Biblica. UK trademark number 1448790.

Scripture quotations marked MSG are taken from *The Message*, copyright © 1993, 1994, 1995, 1996, 2000, 2001, 2002 by
Eugene H. Peterson. Used by permission of NavPress. All rights reserved. Represented by Tyndale House Publishers, Inc.

Pages 8, 127 and 129 – 'On God alone my soul in stillness waits', extract from Psalm 61 from Common Worship is copyright
© The Archbishops' Council, 2000, and is reproduced by permission. All rights reserved. copyright@churchofengland.org.

Every effort has been made to trace and contact copyright owners for material used in this resource. We apologise for any
inadvertent omissions or errors, and would ask those concerned to contact us so that full acknowledgement can be made
in the future.

A catalogue record for this book is available from the British Library

Printed by Gutenberg Press, Tarxien, Malta

GARDEN SONG

Exploring the psalms through paintings, reflections and prayers

Reflections by **Clare Hayns**   Artwork by **Micah Hayns**

Contents

Introduction: Micah 10

Introduction: Clare 12

Psalms of worship

Psalm 19 'The heavens are telling the glory of God' 16

Psalm 33 'Steadfast love… the thoughts of his heart to all generations' 23

Psalm 50 'For every wild animal of the forest is mine' 29

Psalm 96 'Sing to the Lord a new song' 36

Psalm 100 'We are his people and the sheep of his pasture' 42

Psalm 104 'There is the sea, vast and spacious,
teeming with creatures beyond number' 47

Psalm 105 'For he remembered his holy promise, and Abraham, his servant' 54

Psalm 107	'His steadfast love endures forever'	60
Psalm 150	'Let everything that has breath praise the Lord'	67

Psalms of grieving

Psalm 4	'In peace I will lie down and sleep'	74
Psalm 13	'How long must I bear pain in my soul?'	80
Psalm 22	'Save me from the mouth of the lion!'	86
Psalm 25	'He leads the humble in what is right'	93
Psalm 31	'I have become like a broken vessel'	100
Psalm 38	'O my God, do not be far from me'	106
Psalm 39	'While I mused, the fire burned'	112
Psalm 57	'Awake, my soul!'	119
Psalm 62	'On God alone my soul in stillness waits'	126
Psalm 64	'Surely the human mind and heart are cunning'	134

Psalms of joy

Psalm 2	'Therefore, O kings, be wise'	141
Psalm 27	'Behold the beauty of the Lord'	148
Psalm 49	'People, despite their wealth, do not endure'	155
Psalm 71	'Do not cast me off in the time of old age'	162
Psalm 72	'May he be like rain'	169
Psalm 81	'I relieved your shoulder of the burden'	176
Psalm 82	'Give justice to the weak'	183
Psalm 85	'Faithfulness will spring up from the ground'	189
Psalm 87	'All my springs are in you'	196
Psalm 131	'I am like a weaned child with its mother'	202
Psalm 139	'If I take the wings of the morning… even there your hand shall lead me'	208
Notes		215
Space for reflection		217

Introduction: Micah

About five years ago, I was sitting in a Christian conference and was a bit bored with the talk being given. So I decided to flick through my Bible. At that time I was slowly digesting the gospels and hadn't ventured much further than that. But I found myself in the psalms and, more specifically, Psalm 139. I remember reading the verses and feeling so inspired. The visual imagery and emotion were so rich and a stark contrast to the talk I was listening to.

I could see colour and passion in the words. As I read the psalms, they opened up a different side to my faith which I hadn't realised was there. The words didn't feel censored, careful or polite. Instead, they were raw, forward and honest. Having grown up in church environments, I have noticed that sometimes this brash expression of fear, doubt, love and joy can be toned down in worship services. But my inner artist found the psalms to be a deep relief. It felt like the authors were giving me permission to feel and think and fear. I could embrace life in all its fullness and enter into it without the fear of it being too much, too weird, too intense.

This is why I wanted to make this book. I wanted to paint the different verses in the psalms so they might encourage people to read and meditate on them. To find this same freedom and release.

The verse I wrote in a sketchbook during that conference was 'wings of the dawn' (Psalm 139:9, NIV). I saw an image of abundant beauty, colour and life. It was this verse that stayed in my mind and sparked me to take on the project four years later.

I am not sure where the name *Garden Song* came from or when it came to me, but for me it represents the psalms. I like to think of a garden being a metaphor for the kingdom of God, and song being the outward expression of that. As well as this, the word 'psalm' means song.

The pictures are made using either oil paint on canvas or charcoal on paper, using classical techniques I acquired while studying the Old Masters in Florence. I hope you enjoy this book. It was such an honour to create it. All the images are available as prints on my website – **micahhayns.com**. If you could see yourself owning any of the pictures from the book, original pieces and prints are available – please email me at **micah.hayns@gmail.com**.

Micah Hayns

Introduction: Clare

The last time Micah and I collaborated on a book with BRF Ministries (*Unveiled: Women of the Old Testament and the choices they made*), it was very much driven by me; this time it was the other way round. Micah, as he writes in his introduction, felt inspired to paint images from the psalms and asked if I would write reflections to go with these. I am so pleased I agreed, as the process has been a joy and has reignited my love of the psalms.

I have always been drawn to the psalms, as they give voice to the full range of human emotions. I once remember someone saying that the psalms were '150 things it's okay to say to God'. This means they can be uncomfortable to read at times, as they can be angry, despairing and vengeful. For example, Psalm 139 ends with 'I hate them with perfect hatred' (v. 22). The psalmists don't hold back in speaking to God about how they really feel, and this can be enormously refreshing. The psalms can also be glorious songs of praise, containing amazing poetry and imagery, inspiring us to wonder at the world around us and at the faithfulness of God throughout history.

We do not know who wrote the psalms or the exact dates they were written. Some are titled 'of David' or 'of Asaph', but we can't be sure if these were written by them, commissioned by them or inspired by them. Psalms would have been memorised and were used while travelling (the psalms of ascent), in temple liturgy or in private prayer. Jesus drew from the psalms throughout his ministry, and among his final words on the cross were, 'My God, My God, why have you forsaken me' (Psalm 22:1).

Psalms have been used in private and corporate prayer by Christians since the inception of the church. The fourth-century theologian Athanasius wrote:

> Whatever your particular need or trouble, from this same book you can select a form of words to fit it, so that you not merely hear and then pass on, but learn a way to remedy your ill.[1]

The psalms were written to be set to music, and the books of Chronicles refer to psalm singing both inside and outside the temple, normally led by the leaders from the Levite tribe, who were appointed to lead the Israelite community in worship (1 Chronicles 16). We have no idea what this music might have originally sounded like, but psalms have been sung in all forms of musical genre down the centuries: plainchant, choral, hymnody, modern chorus and more. For this reason, we have put together some music for suggested listening, all inspired by the psalms in some way, and from a variety of musical genres. I'd like to thank Alannah, Helen and Katie for help with these. All the music can be found on Spotify (or other sources), and is also available on YouTube. We have also gathered the pieces into a Spotify playlist called 'Garden Song' (**sptfy.com/QRy9**).

I hope that by reading the reflections, looking at Micah's images, and listening to the music you might encounter God within the psalms, and that you might also be inspired to express the full range of human emotions as you do so.

Clare

Clare Hayns

Psalms of worship

16

Psalm 19

'The heavens are telling the glory of God'

The heavens are telling the glory of God,
    and the firmament proclaims his handiwork.
Day to day pours forth speech,
    and night to night declares knowledge.
There is no speech, nor are there words;
    their voice is not heard;
yet their voice goes out through all the earth
    and their words to the end of the world.

In the heavens he has set a tent for the sun,
which comes out like a bridegroom from his wedding canopy,
    and like a strong man runs its course with joy.
Its rising is from the end of the heavens
    and its circuit to the end of them,
    and nothing is hid from its heat.

The law of the Lord is perfect,
    reviving the soul;
the decrees of the Lord are sure,
    making wise the simple;
the precepts of the Lord are right,
    rejoicing the heart;
the commandment of the Lord is clear,
    enlightening the eyes…

Moreover, by them is your servant warned;
    in keeping them there is great reward.
But who can detect one's own errors?
    Clear me from hidden faults.
Keep back your servant also from the insolent;
    do not let them have dominion over me.
Then I shall be blameless
    and innocent of great transgression.

Let the words of my mouth and the meditation of my heart
    be acceptable to you,
    O Lord, my rock and my redeemer.
vv. 1–8, 11–14

In 2023 a new stained-glass window was unveiled in Christ Church Cathedral, Oxford, the first new glass for over 130 years. The window was designed and created by artist John Reyntiens, and at the heart of it is a depiction of St Francis of Assisi, patron saint of animals and the environment. What is striking and unusual about this window is that the image of the saint himself is relatively diminutive in comparison to the vibrant glory of creation all around him. His black and white figure is surrounded by brightly coloured flowers, leaves, birds and bees. The Very Revd Professor Sarah Foot, the dean of Christ Church, says, 'This window reminds us of our responsibilities to care for creation – creation that God made and gave to us to enjoy, but also charged us to look after.'[2]

St Francis believed that nature itself was the mirror of God. He called creatures his 'brothers' and 'sisters' and was said to have preached to the birds. Psalm 19 begins as a song of wonder at creation: 'The heavens are telling the glory of God' (v. 1). Like Francis after him, the psalmist delights in the regular ordering of the days and nights, in the sun which comes up each morning 'like a bridegroom from his wedding canopy' (v. 5).

Thomas Aquinas (c. 1225–74) argued that nature is the first scripture, the Bible the second: 'Sacred writings are bound in two volumes – that of creation and that of Holy Scripture.'[3] The Jewish scribe Ben Sira also connects creation and God's word: 'By the word of the Lord his works are made' (Sirach 42:15).

The second half of the psalm (which some believe may have been two psalms joined together, as the syntax changes in verse 7) moves from praise of creation to praise of God's divine law, which revives the soul, enlightens the eyes and rejoices the heart (vv. 7–8). The law, which was given to Moses and makes up the Torah, is perfect and is to be life-sustaining for all those who can follow it. However, even the psalmist recognises that he is likely to fall short of this perfection, and the psalm moves to be an intimate and personal prayer – 'Clear me from hidden faults' (v. 12).

Christians can pray in awe and wonder at the glory of creation and can appreciate the importance of the Torah, but we believe that Jesus ultimately fulfilled the law, so we don't need to be bound by it in the same way. Read Romans 8 for the apostle Paul's description of this.

As I ponder this psalm, I'm reminded of Jesus, who told his disciples to look to the birds of the air for a reminder of how much they are valued and loved by God:

> Look at the birds of the air: they neither sow nor reap nor gather into barns, and yet your heavenly Father feeds them. Are you not of more value than they?
> MATTHEW 6:26

Jesus used images of the natural world more than anything else in his teaching, pointing to the lilies in the fields, the sheep on the hillside, the figs on a tree.

We can learn so much about God, life, ourselves, by simply going outside for a while, sitting in a garden, listening to birdsong or gazing at a beautiful stained-glass window.

Further reading, reflection and prayer

Reading

> 'Consider the lilies, how they grow: they neither toil nor spin; yet I tell you, even Solomon in all his glory was not clothed like one of these.'
> LUKE 12:27

Listen

'Vivaldi: The Four Seasons, "Spring": I. Allegro' by Nigel Kennedy, English Chamber Orchestra, *Vivaldi: The Four Seasons* (1989)

There are poems that are written for each movement, possibly by Vivaldi himself but no one really knows the author. The poem for spring begins: 'Springtime is upon us. The birds celebrate her return with festive song, and murmuring streams are softly caressed by breezes.'

Prayer

God of all goodness, grant us to desire ardently,
to seek wisely, to know surely, and to accomplish
perfectly your holy will, for the glory of your name.
Thomas Aquinas (c. 1225–74)

23

Psalm 33

'Steadfast love… the thoughts of his heart to all generations'

Rejoice in the Lord, O you righteous.
 Praise befits the upright.
Praise the Lord with the lyre;
 make melody to him with the harp of ten strings…

He loves righteousness and justice;
 the earth is full of the steadfast love of the Lord.

By the word of the Lord the heavens were made
 and all their host by the breath of his mouth.
He gathered the waters of the sea as in a bottle;
 he put the deeps in storehouses.

Let all the earth fear the Lord;
 let all the inhabitants of the world stand in awe of him,

for he spoke, and it came to be;
> he commanded, and it stood firm.

The Lord brings the counsel of the nations to nothing;
> he frustrates the plans of the peoples.

The counsel of the Lord stands forever,
> the thoughts of his heart to all generations.

Happy is the nation whose God is the Lord,
> the people whom he has chosen as his heritage…

Truly the eye of the Lord is on those who fear him,
> on those who hope in his steadfast love…

Our heart is glad in him
> because we trust in his holy name.

Let your steadfast love, O Lord, be upon us,
> even as we hope in you.

vv. 1–2, 5–12, 18, 21–22

My maternal grandfather was a farmer in the Scottish borders, a strong, solid man with working hands, kind eyes and a fondness for snuff and eggnog (both of which are revolting!) By the time I knew him, he'd had a stroke and was pretty much chairbound. Although he found it difficult to speak and move about, he showed love to his grandchildren in numerous little ways – by playing endless games of brick towers; by slowly walking through the farm showing us his land; by patiently listening to us witter on about all sorts of childish nonsense. We felt safe and loved in his presence.

The Hebrew word *hesed* is one of the most beautiful words in scripture. It appears nearly 150 times in the Old Testament, and over 100 of these are in the psalms. It is translated into English in several ways – kindness, mercy, love, loving kindness and as in Psalm 33, steadfast love. It is a word that describes the kind of love my grandfather showed to me.

Hesed is important because it's mainly used in scripture to describe the love God has for humanity. God uses it to describe himself in the moment when he appeared to Moses just before giving the Israelites the covenant and the law:

> The Lord, the Lord, the compassionate and gracious God, slow to anger, abounding in *hesed* and faithfulness, maintaining *hesed* to thousands, and forgiving wickedness, rebellion and sin.
> EXODUS 34:6–7 (NIV)

There are many psalms that remind us of injustice, horror and warfare, which we humans live with and read about each day. This is a psalm to remind us of the 'steadfast love' we've received at certain points in our lives and the impact this has had on us.

Often this will be from those in the generations above us, from grandparents, parents, elderly neighbours and teachers. The actions of others around us that pass from one generation to the next, the little kindnesses shown to one another each day, reflect God's unwavering *hesed*.

Perhaps we can pause to remember those people, to give thanks for their wisdom, kindness and guidance along the way. As we do so, perhaps we can also remember that it all comes from God, who loves us with the same steadfast love that he showed to Moses and all who came after him.

Further reading, reflection and prayer

Reading

'As the Father has loved me, so I have loved you; abide in my love. If you keep my commandments, you will abide in my love, just as I have kept my Father's commandments and abide in his love.'
JOHN 15:9–10

Listen

'Hesed' by Ghost Ship, *Costly*, 2015

Prayer

O God, grant us the spirit of love which does not want to be rewarded, honoured or esteemed, but only to become the blessing and happiness of everything that wants it; love which is the very joy of life.
William Law (1686–1761)

29

Psalm 50

'For every wild animal of the forest is mine'

The mighty one, God the Lord,
    speaks and summons the earth
  from the rising of the sun to its setting.
Out of Zion, the perfection of beauty,
    God shines forth…

'Gather to me my faithful ones,
    who made a covenant with me by sacrifice!'…

Not for your sacrifices do I rebuke you;
    your burnt offerings are continually before me.
I will not accept a bull from your house,
    or goats from your folds.
For every wild animal of the forest is mine,

  the cattle on a thousand hills.
I know all the birds of the air,
  and all that moves in the field is mine.

'If I were hungry, I would not tell you,
  for the world and all that is in it is mine.
Do I eat the flesh of bulls
  or drink the blood of goats?
Offer to God a sacrifice of thanksgiving,
  and pay your vows to the Most High.
Call on me in the day of trouble;
  I will deliver you, and you shall glorify me'…

'Those who bring thanksgiving as their sacrifice honour me;
  to those who go the right way,
  I will show the salvation of God.'
vv. 1–2, 5, 8–15, 23

Years ago, I had a friend who was a great gift-giver. She spent hours deciding on the best and most appropriate presents to give her loved ones. Her gifts weren't always expensive, but you knew they would be creative, thoughtful and just what you wanted (even if you hadn't realised it)! I enjoyed being on the receiving end of her generosity, but I found it somewhat overbearing and dreaded her birthday coming round. I struggled to think of anything particularly interesting to give her, and she often gave me the impression that she was slightly disappointed with my efforts.

Gifts offered in thanks to God have always been an integral part of worship, and in the Old Testament these were often in the form of meat or produce of some kind. People would bring a sacrificial gift if a prayer had been answered, to give thanks for a good harvest or to recognise healing.

If God seems to be silent and distant in so many of our psalms, in this he speaks with utmost, and rather unsettling, clarity: 'Hear, O my people, and I will speak' (v. 7). The issue that the Lord is raising here isn't the quantity or constancy of sacrificial gifts offered at the temple; the concern is the motivation of those bringing them. The gifts seem to be getting ever bigger and more elaborate. Do the people think he will be impressed, or that he needs them, or that these will somehow make him overlook the fact that they behave badly?

> If I were hungry, I would not tell you,
>> for the world and all that is in it is mine.
>
> v. 12

This is a psalm that puts us humans in our rightful place. It is a reminder that God is God and cannot be bribed with gifts or fooled into thinking we are better than we really are because we act in a religious way and say all the right things. It's almost laughable that we ever think in this way, but it's very easy to slip into treating God as if he were a boss we could impress or a friend we could win over with presents.

> These things you have done, and I have been silent;
>> you thought that I was one just like yourself.
>
> v. 21

This psalm is a reminder that the God who created the heavens and earth also knows each and every plant, animal and creature: 'Every wild animal of the forest is mine' (v. 10). God 'knows the secrets of the heart' (Psalm 44:21) and isn't impressed with external signs of religiosity if these aren't paired with living 'the right way' (v. 23). The prophet Micah describes the kind of sacrifice God wants from us – living justly, with kindness and humility. This is the kind of sacrificial gift God desires.

Further reading, reflection and prayer

Reading

> 'Will the Lord be pleased with thousands of rams,
>   with ten thousands of rivers of oil?
> Shall I give my firstborn for my transgression,
>   the fruit of my body for the sin of my soul?'
> He has told you, O mortal, what is good;
>   and what does the Lord require of you
> but to do justice and to love kindness
>   and to walk humbly with your God?
> MICAH 6:7–8

Listen

'Psalm 50' (Aramaic Chant) by Seraphim Bit-Kharibi, *Chanting in the Language of Christ* (2018)

Prayer

Grant me, O Lord, to know what I ought to know,

to love what I ought to love,

to praise what delights thee most,

to value what is precious in thy sight,

to hate what is offensive to thee.

Do not suffer me to judge according to the sight of my eyes,

nor to pass sentence according to the hearing of the ears of ignorant men;

but to discern with a true judgement between things visible and spiritual,

and above all, always to inquire what is the good pleasure of thy will.

Thomas à Kempis (1380–1471)

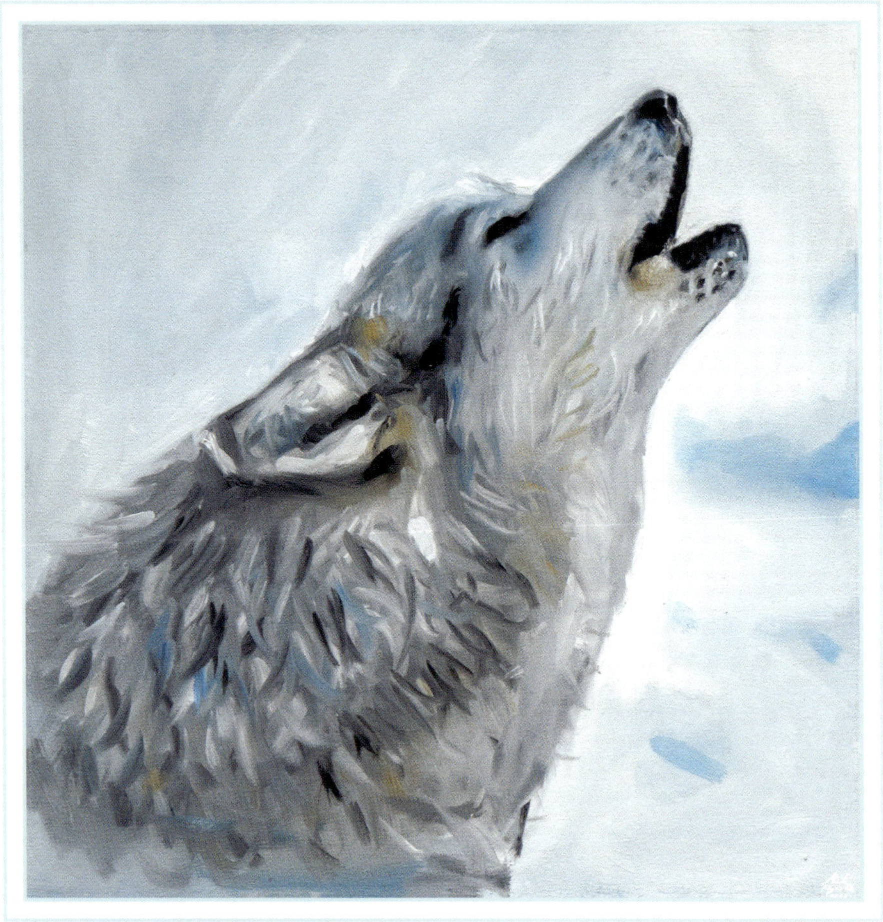

Psalm 96

'Sing to the Lord a new song'

O sing to the Lord a new song;
  sing to the Lord, all the earth.
Sing to the Lord; bless his name;
  tell of his salvation from day to day.
Declare his glory among the nations,
  his marvellous works among all the peoples.
For great is the Lord; and greatly to be praised;
  he is to be revered above all gods.
For all the gods of the peoples are idols,
  but the Lord made the heavens.
Honour and majesty are before him;
  strength and beauty are in his sanctuary.

Ascribe to the Lord, O families of the peoples,
  ascribe to the Lord glory and strength.
Ascribe to the Lord the glory due his name;

>   bring an offering, and come into his courts.
> Worship the Lord in holy splendour;
>   tremble before him, all the earth.
> Say among the nations, 'The Lord is king!
>   The world is firmly established; it shall never be moved.
>   He will judge the peoples with equity.'
> Let the heavens be glad, and let the earth rejoice;
>   let the sea roar and all that fills it;
>   let the field exult and everything in it.
> Then shall all the trees of the forest sing for joy
>   before the Lord, for he is coming,
>   for he is coming to judge the earth.
> He will judge the world with righteousness
>   and the peoples with his truth.

And Mary said,

'My soul magnifies the Lord,
and my spirit rejoices in God my Saviour.'
LUKE 1:46

Mary's song, the Magnificat, is a joyous poem of praise to God. She declares this in the presence of her cousin Elizabeth while they wait for the birth of their children, Jesus and John. Her song echoes Hannah's prayer (1 Samuel 2) when she finds out she is to be having a child (Samuel) after a long and painful wait. Mary recognises the enormity of the task she's been invited to take on as mother to the one who will be the salvation of the world, and her response is to cry out in humble praise 'for the Mighty One has done great things for me' (Luke 1:49).

This psalm calls forth praise from the entirety of creation several times – 'Sing to the Lord', 'Tell of his salvation', 'Declare his glory', and everyone and everything is included, even the earth, the fields, the trees and the sea (vv. 11–12). It's a rapturous song of praise, and it is likely to have been used in the temple liturgy in Jerusalem as part of the autumnal festal celebrations. The psalm calls people to worship and praise, but it also gives reasons why they might 'bless his name'. The reasons include: God is a fair judge (v. 10b); he is the creator (v. 5); he is nothing like the idols some choose to worship (v. 5); and above all 'the Lord is king!' (v. 10).

One of the best things about getting into a habit of reading the psalms every day is that they give us the opportunity to express things to God even when we don't particularly feel like it. There will be occasions when we want to 'sing to the Lord' in an exuberant way like Mary, but there are likely to be more days where we don't have this inclination or desire at all, perhaps because we are finding it hard to see how 'the Lord is king' in the world, in our own life or because we're simply exhausted or not in the mood! A habit of reciting or reading psalms gives us a way of expressing thanksgiving even when we are finding it hard to do so naturally.

When I worked in a cathedral setting, I loved having the opportunity to go to Evensong regularly and hear the choir singing the Magnificat each evening. It was good to end each day remembering Mary's song of joy, and I often found that I was able to remember things to be thankful for as well, even after a hard day's work.

Further reading, reflection and prayer

Reading

Hannah prayed and said,

'My heart exults in the Lord;
    my strength is exalted in my God.
My mouth derides my enemies
    because I rejoice in my victory.'
1 SAMUEL 2:1

Listen

'Magnificat in C' by Charles Villiers Stanford, The King's Consort, Robert King, *I Was Glad* (2013)

Prayer

God, of your goodness give me yourself, for you are sufficient for me. I cannot properly ask anything less, to be worthy of you. If I were to ask less, I should always be in want. In you alone do I have all.

Julian of Norwich (1342—after 1416)

42

Psalm 100

'We are his people and the sheep of his pasture'

Make a joyful noise to the Lord, all the earth.
Serve the Lord with gladness;
   come into his presence with singing.

Know that the Lord is God.
   It is he who made us, and we are his;
   we are his people and the sheep of his pasture.

Enter his gates with thanksgiving
   and his courts with praise.
   Give thanks to him, bless his name.

For the Lord is good;
   his steadfast love endures forever
   and his faithfulness to all generations.

If the psalms contain the entire breadth of human emotion, Psalm 100 is the epitome of joy. 'Make a joyful noise to the Lord', *Jubilate Deo*, is the opening stanza and the setting of some of the most beautiful and uplifting choral pieces ever written. It is a clarion call for the whole earth to cry out and sing praises to God because 'it is he that made us, and we are his' (v. 3).

It is a psalm of belonging, rich with imagery, with the central picture being God as the shepherd taking care of his sheep: 'We are his people, and the sheep of his pasture' (v. 3). All the biblical patriarchs, and many of the kings and prophets, were shepherds by trade. The local area was perfect for grazing, and the early Israelite communities depended on sheep farming for their subsistence, so it's not surprising that shepherding has been used as an enduring image for God's love. I confess I've often found the metaphor difficult. It's hard to think of being compared to a sheep as a particularly favourable image: sheep aren't the brightest of God's creatures and, unless you spend an awful lot of time with them, most people would be hard pushed to distinguish one from another!

This isn't a psalm about sheep, though, and it's not really about us either; it's about God. I find that a huge relief. There are times when it's good to turn our focus away from ourselves and our own troubles, whatever they might be, and simply turn to God and be thankful. Sometimes I find music helps as it can transport me to a place where I can forget all the things I'm striving for or worried about for a moment.

When we praise God like this all we need to know is 'the Lord is God' (v. 2), 'the Lord is good' (v. 5) and that we belong to him (v. 3). There is a time for theological debate, for our worries and troubles, but there is also a time when we are invited to put that aside and allow ourselves to be carried and cared for, just as the shepherd cares for his sheep. In John's gospel, Jesus, the good shepherd, protects his sheep from harm, knows each one by name and lays down his life for them (John 10).

That's something to be joyful about.

Further reading, reflection and prayer

Reading

'I am the good shepherd. The good shepherd lays down his life for the sheep. The hired hand, who is not the shepherd and does not own the sheep, sees the wolf coming and leaves the sheep and runs away, and the wolf snatches them and scatters them. The hired hand runs away because a hired hand does not care for the sheep. I am the good shepherd. I know my own, and my own know me, just as the Father knows me, and I know the Father. And I lay down my life for the sheep.'
JOHN 10:11–15

Listen

'All people that on earth do dwell ("Old 100th")' by Ralph Vaughan Williams, The Choir of Westminster Abbey, *The Queen's Diamond Jubilee – Royal Music from Westminster Abbey* (2012)

Prayer

The Lord, ye know is God indeed;
without our aid he did us make;
we are his folk, he doth us feed,
and for his sheep he doth us take.

O enter then his gates with praise,
approach with joy his courts unto;
praise, laud and bless his name always,
for it is seemly so to do.
William Kethe (d. 1594)

47

Psalm 104

'There is the sea, vast and spacious, teeming with creatures beyond number'

Praise the Lord, my soul.

Lord my God, you are very great;
> you are clothed with splendour and majesty…

The trees of the Lord are well watered,
> the cedars of Lebanon that he planted.

There the birds make their nests;
> the stork has its home in the junipers.

The high mountains belong to the wild goats;
> the crags are a refuge for the hyrax.

He made the moon to mark the seasons,
> and the sun knows when to go down.

You bring darkness, it becomes night,
    and all the beasts of the forest prowl.
The lions roar for their prey
    and seek their food from God.
The sun rises, and they steal away;
    they return and lie down in their dens.
Then people go out to their work,
    to their labour until evening.

How many are your works, Lord!
    In wisdom you made them all;
    the earth is full of your creatures.
There is the sea, vast and spacious,
    teeming with creatures beyond number –
    living things both large and small.
There the ships go to and fro,
    and Leviathan, which you formed to frolic there…

I will sing to the Lord all my life;
    I will sing praise to my God as long as I live.

Praise the Lord, my soul.
vv. 1, 16–26, 33 (NIV)

There are times when it's good and right to stop and simply wonder at the sheer beauty of this earth we live in, and this psalm is a reminder to do just that. 'Praise the Lord, my soul' is uttered at the beginning (v. 1) and at the end (v. 35), and everything in between is the psalmist wondering at the sheer awesomeness of creation.

This is a psalm where humankind is reminded that it's not all about us! In fact, people are hardly mentioned except in the context of work (v. 23) and in the fact the earth provides for us (vv. 14–15); the rest of the psalm is about everything else. It's about the innumerable creeping things, the young lions hunting for prey, the springs that provide water for animals, the vast monsters of the seas and the trees which shelter the birds.

It's a reminder of creation as it should be and perhaps once was, where everything is of value, where there is a right order and each creature has enough.

We are, let's hope, beginning to wake up to the fact that we are on the cusp of an environmental catastrophe. Sir David Attenborough, surely the most brilliant evangelist of our time for the conservation of our natural world, says:

> We now have a few short years during which we can still make a choice. Where just enough remains of the natural world for it to recover. This starts and ends with us.[4]

Attenborough's recent documentary *Wild Isles* focuses on the British Isles, and it's astonishing to see the beauty of these small islands with their grasslands, woodlands, oceans and rivers. However, the statistics are stark – 30 million birds have vanished from our skies in the last 50 years, 97% of wildflower meadows have disappeared since the 1930s and one quarter of all our mammals are at risk of extinction – and this is just in Great Britain.

We no longer believe in a three-tiered creation as the psalmist did, with God dwelling in the heavens above us, but we can agree that we live on a remarkable planet and surely need to do everything we can to protect it for future generations.

In the diocese of Oxford there has been a recent revision to the liturgy of baptism and confirmation services to include a new final question at the end, where the whole congregation is invited to makes a promise:

> Will you strive to safeguard the integrity of creation, and sustain and renew the life of the earth?
> All: With the help of God, I will.

Surely that is something we can all proclaim.

Further reading, reflection and prayer

Reading

> And God said, 'Let the waters bring forth swarms of living creatures, and let birds fly above the earth across the dome of the sky.' So God created the great sea monsters and every living creature that moves, of every kind, with which the waters swarm and every winged bird of every kind. And God saw that it was good. God blessed them, saying, 'Be fruitful and multiply and fill the waters in the seas, and let birds multiply on the earth.' And there was evening and there was morning, the fifth day.
> GENESIS 1:20–23

Listen

'What a Wonderful World' by Louis Armstrong, *What a Wonderful World* (1968)

Prayer

We pray to God our creator:

for the earth itself, that it may sustain future generations;

for the creatures of the earth, the animals and plants, the seas and oceans, and forests;

for humanity, made in God's image, gifted so richly and flawed so deeply.

Good Lord, we pray. Amen.

54

Psalm 105

'For he remembered his holy promise and Abraham, his servant'

O give thanks to the Lord; call on his name;
   make known his deeds among the peoples.
Sing to him, sing praises to him;
   tell of all his wonderful works.
Glory in his holy name;
   let the hearts of those who seek the Lord rejoice.
Seek the Lord and his strength;
   seek his presence continually.
Remember the wonderful works he has done,
   his miracles and the judgements he has uttered,
O offspring of his servant Abraham,
   children of Jacob, his chosen ones.

> He is the Lord our God;
>   his judgements are in all the earth.
> He is mindful of his covenant forever,
>   of the word that he commanded, for a thousand generations,
> the covenant that he made with Abraham,
>   his sworn promise to Isaac,
> which he confirmed to Jacob as a statute,
>   to Israel as an everlasting covenant,
> saying, 'To you I will give the land of Canaan
>   as your portion for an inheritance'…
> For he remembered his holy promise
>   and Abraham, his servant.
>
> vv. 1–11, 42

Sharing stories is an important part of being human. It is the oldest form of communication. Our brains are hardwired for it, and a good story can make us angry, upset or empathetic. It can lead us to action or reduce us to tears. Our novelists, playwrights and cinema producers know the power of story to transform and bring about change, and dictators and tyrants similarly use stories to entice and manipulate. Margaret Atwood, who is a wonderful storyteller, says that humans evolved into being storytellers:

> Once we had a language that included a past and a present and the future, once we could think about what had happened and transfer information to people about what might therefore happen, we were going to be telling stories.[5]

There is something very human about gathering in a group to tell stories. As a university chaplain I had the privilege of hosting interesting talks and dinners, and one of my favourite events was a regular inter-faith gathering which brought together students from the Jewish, Muslim and Christian communities alongside their respective chaplains. The aim was to get to know one another, share stories and food, and at times we studied the scriptures together to find points of connection, one of those being the importance of Abraham to all our respective faiths.

Psalm 105 is a historical psalm which tells the story of God's faithfulness, touching on many of the wonderful stories of scripture from Genesis to Exodus. It begins with thankfulness, 'O give thanks to the Lord; call on his name' (v. 1), and then moves into describing why there might be reasons to be thankful. The reasons aren't personal, but historical, beginning with the covenant promise God made to Abraham, Isaac and Jacob (vv. 9–10), and then telling the story of how God protected the people from famine through Joseph (v. 23), released them from captivity at the time of Moses and Aaron (v. 26) and provided for them in the wilderness years (vv. 40–42).

Many of us are less confident when it comes to reading the Hebrew scriptures than we are with the New Testament. The stories can seem remote, distant and confusing; at times they can seem overly violent; and the promise of land for a chosen people sits uncomfortably when we consider the complex political situation in modern-day Israel and Palestine. Having said that, I strongly believe that having a good understanding of the stories of the patriarchs and prophets of old helps us to make sense of our present faith.

Once a year our wider family gathers for a few days' holiday together and one of the traditions we have is to go round and think of one thing we're thankful for from the year that's past and one thing we're hopeful for in the year to come. It's a way to share our stories of the past year and to listen to one another, and it also helps us make sense of where we are in the present. When times are tough it can be good to zoom out and see things from a wider perspective. This psalm helps us to do that – the God who made a promise to be faithful to father Abraham all those centuries ago is the same God who will be faithful to us today. Praise the Lord!

Further reading, reflection and prayer

Reading

This is a moment to go to the Bible and read your favourite story from scripture. Mine is the story of the five daughters of Zelophehad who changed Moses' mind (Numbers 27).

Listen

'Manna (After All These Years)' by Chris Renzema, *Manna Pt.1* (2023)

Prayer

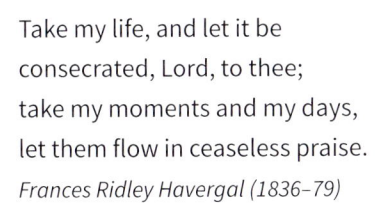

Take my life, and let it be
consecrated, Lord, to thee;
take my moments and my days,
let them flow in ceaseless praise.
Frances Ridley Havergal (1836–79)

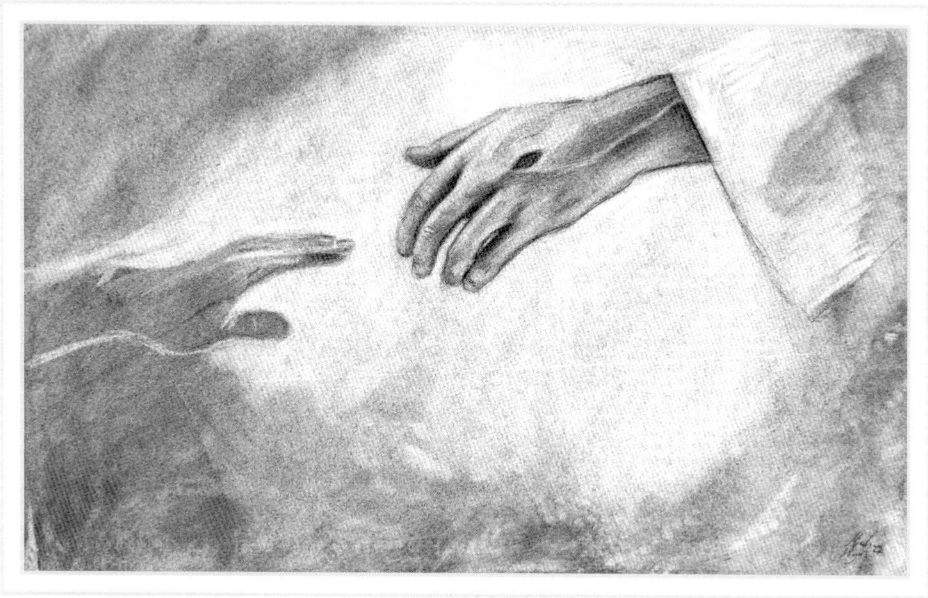

Psalm 107

'His steadfast love endures forever'

O give thanks to the Lord, for he is good,
  for his steadfast love endures forever…

Some wandered in desert wastes,
  finding no way to an inhabited town;
hungry and thirsty,
  their soul fainted within them.
Then they cried to the Lord in their trouble,
  and he delivered them from their distress…

Some sat in darkness and in gloom,
  prisoners in misery and in irons…
Their hearts were bowed down with hard labour;
  they fell down, with no one to help.
Then they cried to the Lord in their trouble,
  and he saved them from their distress…

Some went down to the sea in ships,
    doing business on the mighty waters;
they saw the deeds of the Lord,
    his wondrous works in the deep.
For he commanded and raised the stormy wind,
    which lifted up the waves of the sea.
They mounted up to heaven; they went down to the depths;
    their courage melted away in their calamity;
they reeled and staggered like drunkards
    and were at their wits' end.
Then they cried to the Lord in their trouble,
    and he brought them out from their distress;
he made the storm be still,
    and the waves of the sea were hushed.
Then they were glad because they had quiet,
    and he brought them to their desired haven.
Let them thank the Lord for his steadfast love,
    for his wonderful works to humankind...

Let those who are wise pay attention to these things.
vv. 1, 4–6, 10, 12–13, 23–31, 43

'HIS STEADFAST LOVE ENDURES FOREVER' 63

The refrain throughout this psalm, repeated six times in various ways, is 'Thank the Lord for his steadfast love.' To be steadfast is to be firm, unwavering and unfailing, and this psalm is a reminder of all the ways in which God has reached out to his people with steadfast love.

The main section of the psalm follows a simple pattern, giving four scenarios of people who needed help and salvation. There are those who got lost in the wilderness (vv. 4–6), those who were in the darkness of prison (vv. 10–12), those who were sick (or foolish, depending on the translation) because of some kind of sinful behaviour (vv. 17–18), and finally those who were trapped in storms at sea (vv. 23–26). Each time the people cried out to God, and immediately they were saved: the lost were led to straight paths (v. 7); the prisoners were released (v. 14); the sick were healed (v. 20); and the storms were stilled (v. 29). No wonder the people were able to rejoice and thank the Lord!

The problem with this, though, is that it doesn't match up with reason or experience. We can all think of times and situations when we've cried out to God but our prayers don't seem to be answered. Not everyone finds themself on the straight path; there are millions who are unjustly imprisoned; sick people are not all healed; and just today I read of a ship full of men who drowned at sea trying to reach safety.

Walter Brueggemann, in his book *Spirituality of the Psalms,* describes this type of psalm as one of 'orientation' and points out that it violates our rationality as 'rhetoric that defies reason'. Brueggemann points out the dichotomy between acknowledging and giving thanks for God's faithfulness, symmetry and provision, but also recognising that 'life is also savagely masked by incoherence, a loss of balance and unrelieved asymmetry'.[6]

The psalmist reminds us to look back into history and remember all the ways in which God has indeed saved his people. The whole arc of the Judeo-Christian story is of God delivering his people from captivity into freedom, be that from Egypt, Babylon, sin or death. The climax of this arc of salvation was fully realised in Jesus, who showed us through his life, death and resurrection what 'steadfast love' really looks like.

There are many things we won't understand, not least why God seems to intervene in some situations and not others, and we would be foolish to think everything can be simply explained anyway.

The psalm ends with 'let those who are wise pay attention to these things' (v. 43). So perhaps in these situations the only wise thing to do is to 'thank the Lord for his steadfast love'.

Further reading, reflection and prayer

Reading

> But God, who is rich in mercy, out of the great love with which he loved us even when we were dead through our trespasses, made us alive together with Christ – by grace you have been saved.
> EPHESIANS 2:4–5

Listen

'Nimrod from Enigma Variations' by Edward Elgar, Royal Philharmonic Orchestra, *Last Night of the Proms* (2007)

Prayer

Grant us, O Lord our God, ever to find in thee a very present help in times of trouble. When we are in the darkness of doubt or perplexity, shed thy light upon our way. When we are burdened with the affairs of our daily life, lift us to the calm of thy presence. When we are battling with temptation and the flesh is weak, by the light of thy Spirit make us strong to overcome. We ask these things through him in whom we are more than conquerors, thy Son Jesus Christ our Lord. Amen.

St Anselm (d. 1109)

67

Psalm 150

'Let everything that has breath praise the Lord'

Praise the Lord.

Praise God in his sanctuary;
   praise him in his mighty heavens.
Praise him for his acts of power;
   praise him for his surpassing greatness.
Praise him with the sounding of the trumpet,
   praise him with the harp and lyre,
praise him with tambourine and dancing,
   praise him with the strings and pipe,

praise him with the clash of cymbals,
>   praise him with resounding cymbals.

Let everything that has breath praise the Lord.

Praise the Lord.
(NIV)

When my children were little, we used to go to a toddler music group and at the end of the session all the toddlers were given different instruments – drums, tambourines, cymbals and recorders – and they could just let rip. As you can imagine, it was ear-achingly loud! This final psalm ends in a cacophony of praise with a whole variety of instruments being played all at once to create what I imagine to be a similarly loud, but perhaps more tuneful, noise.

The book of Psalms has moved us through a whole gamut of human emotion and experience. The first half of the book is dominated by songs of prayer, pleading and protest, whereas in the second half psalms of praise become more prominent. However, there is no other psalm quite like this final one, which is just pure, unalloyed, unadulterated praise.

It is as if all the pain, abandonment, conflict, suffering and confusion have been put to one side, and all that is left is praise, a word that is used thirteen times in just six verses. There is a sense that it's not just humans who should praise God, but all of creation:

> Let everything that has breath praise the Lord.
> v. 6 (NIV)

I love a party and am never happier than when surrounded by my family and closest friends, with some good music, a few disco lights and some space to dance. In those moments it feels as if all my troubles melt away for a while. This may not be to everyone's taste, and a party like this might evoke memories of terrible dancing and awkward encounters. This psalm evokes a different kind of party, the one that is in heaven, where 'Death will be no more; mourning and crying and pain will be no more' (Revelation 21:4) and where there will be eternal and unstoppable joy, peace, goodness and praise. This psalm is a conclusion, not just because it is the final one, but also because everything ultimately concludes in the joy of eternity.

We are not there yet, of course, but we are given glimpses of heaven every now and then, and the invitation is to notice and to give thanks to God for them. And one way to do this is to lift our voice in worship and praise. Augustine of Hippo wrote that 'to sing is to pray twice', and John Wesley wrote: 'Sing all… Sing lustily and with good courage… above all sing spiritually (having) an eye to God in every word you sing.'[7]

Praise the Lord! Take a moment to be thankful to God, even, in the same vein as this psalm, perhaps thinking of 13 different things to praise God for!

Further reading, reflection and prayer

Reading

> After this I heard what seemed to be the loud voice of a great multitude in heaven, saying, 'Hallelujah! Salvation and glory and power to our God…'
>
> And from the throne came a voice saying, 'Praise our God, all you his servants, and all who fear him, small and great.'
> REVELATION 19:1, 5

Listen

This joyful version of Psalm 150 is sung in Hebrew and performed by an Israeli band.

'Halleluhu (Psalm 150)' by Miqedem, *Miqedem* (2016)

Prayer

Great, O Lord, is your kingdom, your power and your glory;
great also is your wisdom, your goodness, your justice,
   your mercy;
and for all these we bless you, and will magnify your name
   forever and ever.
George Wither (1588–1667)

Psalms of grieving

74

Psalm 4

'In peace I will lie down and sleep'

Answer me when I call to you,
 my righteous God.
Give me relief from my distress;
 have mercy on me and hear my prayer.

How long will you people turn my glory into shame?
 How long will you love delusions and seek false gods?
Know that the Lord has set apart his faithful servant for himself;
 the Lord hears when I call to him.

Tremble and do not sin;
 when you are on your beds,
 search your hearts and be silent.
Offer the sacrifices of the righteous
 and trust in the Lord.

> Many, Lord, are asking, 'Who will bring us prosperity?'
>   Let the light of your face shine on us.
> Fill my heart with joy
>   when their grain and new wine abound.
>
> In peace I will lie down and sleep,
>   for you alone, Lord,
>   make me dwell in safety.
> (NIV)

The book of Psalms is the hymnbook of the Bible, with poetry and verse that form the basis of many of the hymns and songs that we sing in our churches today. We are likely to have heard of Isaac Watts, John Newton and Charles Wesley, but one of the most significant American hymnodists, who penned over 9,000 hymns in her lifetime, was a blind woman from New York called Fanny Crosby. Born in 1820, she was clearly a genius, writing her first poem at eight years old and performing in the White House in her early 20s. She was so prolific she had to use multiple pseudonyms to be taken seriously, as she often wrote up to seven hymns in a day.

Her hymns include the well-known 'To God be the glory' and 'Blessed assurance', but the first one ever published was 'An Evening Hymn', based on verse 8 of this psalm.

The first verse reads:

> Once more at rest, my peaceful thoughts are blending,
> Once more, O Lord, Thy loving smile I see;
> For softly now the twilight shades descending
> Have closed, and left my heart alone with Thee.
> *'An Evening Hymn' by Fanny Crosby (1853)*

This psalm is unusual as it's not primarily addressing God, other than the first verse, but other people. The psalmist is frustrated that his fellow humans are looking for answers in all the wrong places – 'How long will you love delusions and seek false gods?' (v. 2). He compares this with his own realisation that striving after 'grain or new wine' (or whatever it is we now yearn for) isn't comparable to having a heart filled with the joy that comes from being content and safe with God.

When we put our head on the pillow at night, we can often find ourselves worrying about the day that's past, thinking of all the things we haven't achieved, all the things we've got wrong or about the day to come, fretting about a work problem or a tricky conversation we need to have. As we get older, sleep can become even more restless, and we can only look in envy at the deep, trouble-free sleep of a baby.

Psalm 4 is often prayed at the night-time service of Compline as it reminds us that, whatever the stresses and strains of the past day, we can be at peace and 'lie down and sleep, for you alone, Lord, make me dwell in safety' (v. 8). I find the Ignatian prayer of the Examen helpful at the end of the day, where you prayerfully recall all the good, Godly moments (consolation), alongside all the times where God has seemed absent (desolation) and, without judgement, hold them all up in prayer. A key part of the practice is reflecting on the day and learning to see it as Jesus did. The hope is that, over time, these patterns might also help us become aware of a particular calling that maybe we didn't see so clearly before.[8]

The refrain of Crosby's 'An Evening Hymn' is:

> Still, still I hear Thy words of consolation
> That gave me hope when I was sorely tried;
> And since that hour of hallowed meditation,
> Thy counsel, Lord, has been my only guide.

Further reading, reflection and prayer

Reading

'Come away to a deserted place all by yourselves and rest a while.' For many were coming and going, and they had no leisure even to eat.
MARK 6:31

Listen

'An Evening Hymn' by Emma Kirkby St Alban's Chamber Choir, *Baroque Vocal Masterpieces* (2014)

Prayer

Drop thy still dews of quietness,
till all our strivings cease;
take from our souls the strain and stress,
and let our ordered lives confess
the beauty of thy peace.
John Greenleaf Whittier (1807–92)

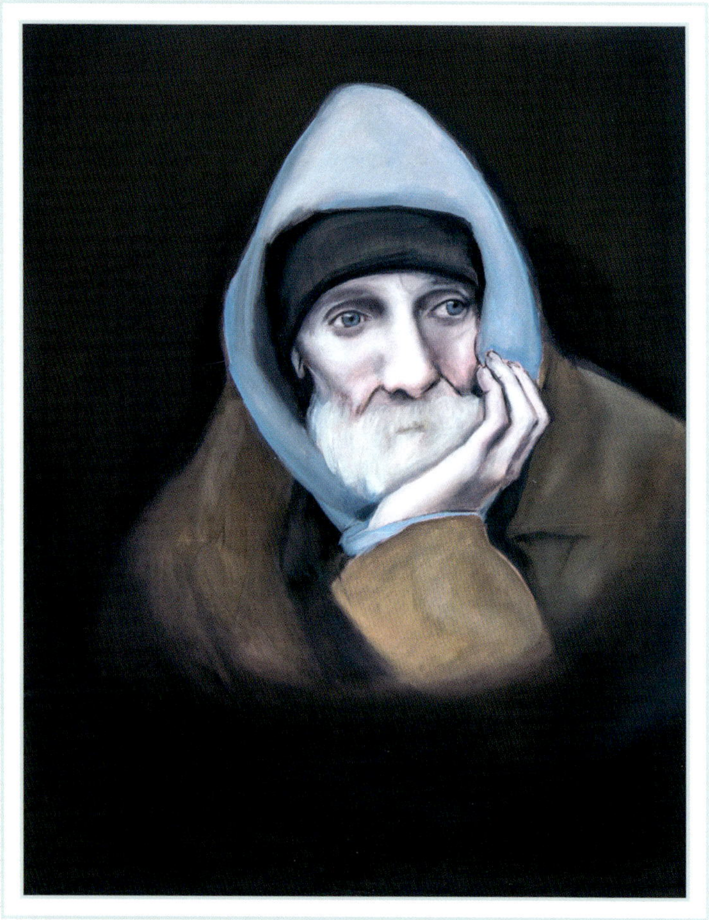

Psalm 13

'How long must I bear pain in my soul?'

How long, O Lord? Will you forget me forever?
  How long will you hide your face from me?
How long must I bear pain in my soul
  and have sorrow in my heart all day long?
How long shall my enemy be exalted over me?

Consider and answer me, O Lord my God!
  Give light to my eyes, or I will sleep the sleep of death,
and my enemy will say, 'I have prevailed';
  my foes will rejoice because I am shaken.

But I trusted in your steadfast love;
  my heart shall rejoice in your salvation.
I will sing to the Lord
  because he has dealt bountifully with me.

How long, how long, how long, how long?

A fourfold plea begins this psalm of lament. It is the cry of someone who is not only in deep distress, but whose pain has been enduring for a long time. This is a psalm for those who have struggled for years with no let-up; for those who experience chronic pain; for those who have been bullied; for those who feel God has abandoned them in their struggle; for all who have prayed for a particular person or situation but haven't had the answer they have longed for. Many of us will, at some point in our lives, cry out, 'How long, O Lord?'

A friend of mine recently shared with me that his father had lived with dementia for the past decade, slowly declining from being a sharp and astute accountant to the point where he repeated his name over and over again to remember who he was. In recent months he had been unable to recognise his own name, his wife of 50 years or his five children. The whole family were exhausted and were wondering where God was in all of it:

> How long will you hide your face from me?
> v. 1

A parishioner of mine struggled with chronic depression for years, and this prevented them from being able to work and look after their family in the way they would have liked. At times there were periods when even getting out of bed was too much, causing them deep distress and pain:

> How long must I wrestle with my thoughts
>   and day after day have sorrow in my heart?
> v. 2 (NIV)

Another friend experienced significant bullying and harassment after making a legitimate complaint at work, and this led to a long period of conflict which became hard to disentangle from:

> How long shall my enemy be exalted over me?
> v. 2

The psalmist's plaintive cry turns to prayer as he asks God for three things: to be seen, to be heard and for there to be hope: 'Consider and answer me… Give light to my eyes' (v. 3).

As the psalm goes on, something shifts and changes, and by the end there are glimmers of hope. We can't know what brings about this transformation, but somehow there is the realisation that underpinning everything is 'steadfast love' and that because of this love 'my heart rejoices' and it becomes possible once again to sing and to hope (vv. 5–6).

It's too simplistic to say that if we just pray and trust in God's love then everything will be alright, and I'm sure we all know situations where this hasn't been the case. We are not promised protection from hardship, but the Christian hope is that pain, suffering and even death itself are not the end of the story. The good news, and it really is Good News, is that we are accompanied through these tough times by Jesus Christ, who embodied steadfast love and walked the ultimate path of pain into eternal life.

Sometimes we need to dwell for a while in a state of lament, expressing our pain before God. This psalm gives us permission to do just that.

Further reading, reflection and prayer

Reading

> For everything there is a season and a time for every matter under heaven…
> a time to weep and a time to laugh; a time to mourn and a time to dance.
> ECCLESIASTES 3:1, 4

Listen

'How Long?' by Bifrost Arts, *Lamentations: Simple songs of lament and hope, vol. 1* (2016)

Prayer

Christ be with me, Christ within me,
Christ behind me, Christ before me,
Christ beside me, Christ to win me,
Christ to comfort and restore me,
Christ beneath me, Christ above me,
Christ in quiet, Christ in danger,
Christ in hearts of all that love me,
Christ in mouth of friend and stranger.
St Patrick

86

Psalm 22

'Save me from the mouth of the lion!'

My God, my God, why have you forsaken me?
Why are you so far from helping me, from the words of my groaning?
O my God, I cry by day, but you do not answer;
   and by night but find no rest…

But I am a worm and not human,
   scorned by others and despised by the people.
All who see me mock me;
   they sneer at me; they shake their heads;
'Commit your cause to the Lord; let him deliver –
   let him rescue the one in whom he delights!'

Yet it was you who took me from the womb;
   you kept me safe on my mother's breast.

On you I was cast from my birth,
    and since my mother bore me you have been my God.
Do not be far from me,
    for trouble is near,
    and there is no one to help…

They open wide their mouths at me,
    like a ravening and roaring lion…

Deliver my soul from the sword,
    my life from the power of the dog!
    Save me from the mouth of the lion!…

From you comes my praise in the great congregation;
    my vows I will pay before those who fear him.
The poor shall eat and be satisfied;
    those who seek him shall praise the Lord.
    May your hearts live forever!

All the ends of the earth shall remember
    and turn to the Lord.

vv. 1–2, 6–11, 13, 20–21, 25–27

No one was there to witness the actual moment of the resurrection, when Jesus' soul was restored to his broken body and he rose up, pushed away the hard, grey rock and walked out of the mouth of the tomb. We know it happened because of the numerous people who encountered him, be it in the garden or the upper room or walking on the road to Emmaus, and because terrified disciples were transformed into fearless apostles and lives were changed.

This is one of the psalms of lament which were regularly prayed by the people of ancient Israel to express their feelings of helplessness and frustration to God; sometimes they are even frustrated with God: 'I cry by day, but you do not answer; and by night but find no rest' (v. 2).

This is the psalm Jesus goes to at his time of most desperate need, when he cried out in his mother tongue, Aramaic, from the horror of the cross:

> 'Eli, Eli, lema sabachthani?' that is, 'My God, my God, why have you forsaken me?'
> MATTHEW 27:46

This psalm is often read at Good Friday, and it's hard to read it without recalling the crucifixion, as we remember Jesus who was mocked, abandoned, beaten and killed. Although this psalm is a lament, it also expresses deep faith in the midst of trial. When read carefully we see there is a turning point, a moment of transformation, which comes between the two stanzas of verse 21:

> Save me from the mouth of the lion!
> From the horns of the wild oxen you have rescued me.

What changed between those two lines? We don't get to find out, but whatever happened the psalmist is transformed. They are no longer lonely and isolated but are within their community once again (v. 22); they have stopped thinking only of themselves and are now considering the needy (v. 26); and they are able to praise God once again (v. 25). The psalmist doesn't give up or doubt God's presence, but they look back and remember how God has been faithful in the past (v. 4), has known them from birth (v. 9), and has been with them throughout their life (v. 10).

There are times in our lives when God seems far off, all our prayers seem to drift into an empty void, and we wonder if anyone is out there at all. And then something shifts in us. We can't quite put a finger on what has changed, but we feel hopeful again; it's as if the first signs of spring have appeared after a long and bleak winter.

This is the crux of the Christian story of resurrection hope – where lives are transformed from despair to hope, from darkness to light, from the mouth of lions to the arms of the one who has known us ever since we were in the womb (v. 9).

Further reading, reflection and prayer

Reading

> Blessed be the God and Father of our Lord Jesus Christ, the Father of mercies and the God of all consolation, who consoles us in all our affliction, so that we may be able to console those who are in any affliction with the consolation with which we ourselves are consoled by God.
> 2 CORINTHIANS 1:3–4

Listen

'From Jewish life, B.55: I. Prayer' by Ernest Bloch, Sol Gabetta, *Prayer* (2014)

Prayer

Lord Jesus Christ, we thank you
for all the benefits that you have won for us,
for all the pains and insults that you have borne for us.
Most merciful redeemer, friend and brother,
may we know you more clearly,
love you more dearly,
and follow you more nearly, day by day.

St Richard of Chichester (1197–1253)

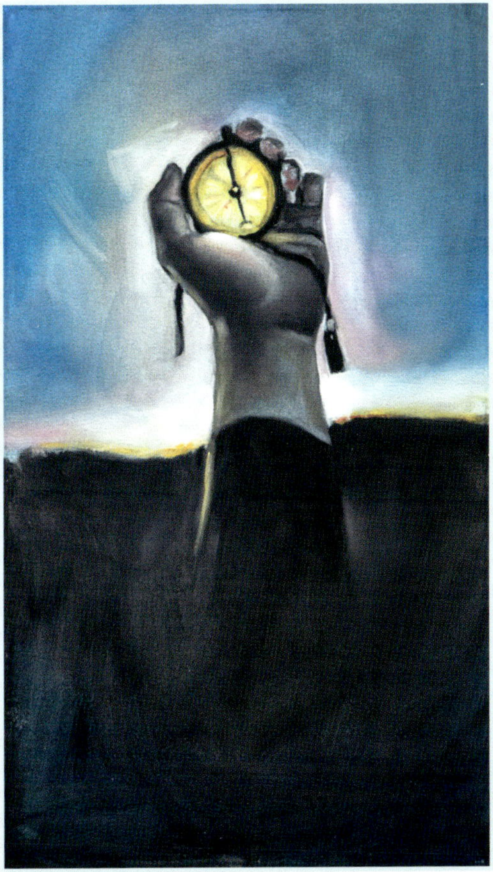

Psalm 25

'He leads the humble in what is right'

To you, O Lord, I lift up my soul.
O my God, in you I trust;
  do not let me be put to shame;
  do not let my enemies exult over me.
Do not let those who wait for you be put to shame;
  let them be ashamed who are wantonly treacherous.

Make me to know your ways, O Lord;
  teach me your paths.
Lead me in your truth and teach me,
  for you are the God of my salvation;
  for you I wait all day long.

> Be mindful of your mercy, O Lord, and of your steadfast love,
>   for they have been from of old.
> Do not remember the sins of my youth or my transgressions;
>   according to your steadfast love remember me,
>   for the sake of your goodness, O Lord!
>
> Good and upright is the Lord;
>   therefore he instructs sinners in the way.
> He leads the humble in what is right
>   and teaches the humble his way.
> All the paths of the Lord are steadfast love and faithfulness,
>   for those who keep his covenant and his decrees.
>
> For your name's sake, O Lord,
>   pardon my guilt, for it is great.
> Who are they that fear the Lord?
>   He will teach them the way that they should choose.
>
> vv. 1–12

The psalmist David lived through numerous conflicts and times of turbulence during his long and varied life. From the moment he took five stones when he was 'little more than a boy' (1 Samuel 17:42, NIV) and defeated the monstrous Goliath, he was almost constantly in conflict of some kind. He endured the rages of King Saul, which were so violent he once had to flee out of a window (1 Samuel 19:12); as king he led countless battles to conquer Jerusalem (2 Samuel 5); and even towards the end of his life he was at war with his own son, Absalom, who tried to overthrow him (2 Samuel 15—18). It is likely that this psalm was written in later life – 'Do not remember the sins of my youth' (v. 7) and so it may have been this last conflict that David was referring to when he says, 'Let them be ashamed who are wantonly treacherous' (v. 3).

Every spring, I go with a group of friends on a mini-pilgrimage. We normally pick a waymarked route, such as St Hilda's Way in Yorkshire or the North Wales Pilgrim's Way, and follow the signs to our chosen destination. We once tried to walk a route that we had planned ourselves, and it was enormously stressful and led to us getting lost several times a day. From then on, we always pick a route where we can rely on the signs pointing us in the right direction.[9]

This psalm is a prayer for guidance and direction ('Make me to know your ways… teach me your paths. Lead me', vv. 4–5), something we all long for at some time or other. Making decisions about the direction of our lives can be hard at the best of times, but during times of conflict or turmoil this becomes even more difficult. How can we be sure we are following God's paths for our lives? How do we know if we have wandered off? Why aren't the signs more obvious?

I don't have a simple answer; however, the psalmist notes that 'all the paths of the Lord are steadfast love and faithfulness' (v. 10), so perhaps this gives us some clues. King David certainly didn't always make the right decisions throughout his life. His decision to send Bathsheba's husband, Uriah, to the frontline of battle in the hope that he would be killed so he could acquire his wife was one of his worst (see Psalm 51) – this may be what he was referring to by 'the sins of my youth'. Perhaps we know when we are on the right path by the signs of love and faithfulness that we find there?

I enjoy reading the psalms in different translations, and Megan Daffern's translation is excellent; her version of verse 15 uses the phrase 'tangled up' when talking about our footsteps.[10] We can all get rather 'tangled up' at times, finding we're lost and realising we need a bit of help navigating back onto the right path.

There is a humility in asking for guidance – many people hate even asking for simple directions, let alone asking for help and support when it comes to the big decisions in life! Prayer is a humble action, as when we pray, we are acknowledging that we can't do it on our own and we need God.

> He leads the humble in what is right
>   and teaches the humble his way.
> v. 9

Further reading, reflection and prayer

Reading

> If my people who are called by my name humble themselves, pray, seek my face, and turn from their wicked ways, then I will hear from heaven and will forgive their sin and heal their land. Now my eyes will be open and my ears attentive to the prayer that is made in this place.
> 2 CHRONICLES 7:14–15

Listen

'Remember Me' by The Porter's Gate, *Sanctuary Songs* (2023)

Prayer

Forgive me my sins, O Lord;
forgive me the sins of my youth and of my age,
the sins of my soul and the sins of my body,
my secret and my whispering sins,
my presumptuous and my crying sins,
the sins I have done to please myself
and the sins I have done to please others.
Forgive me the sins which I know,
and those sins which I know not:
forgive them, O Lord
forgive them of thy great goodness.

Lancelot Andrewes (1555–1626)

100

Psalm 31

'I have become like a broken vessel'

You are indeed my rock and my fortress;
    for your name's sake lead me and guide me;
take me out of the net that is hidden for me,
    for you are my refuge.
Into your hand I commit my spirit;
    you have redeemed me, O Lord, faithful God…

Be gracious to me, O Lord, for I am in distress;
    my eye wastes away from grief,
    my soul and body also.
For my life is spent with sorrow,
    and my years with sighing;
my strength fails because of my misery,
    and my bones waste away.

> I am the scorn of all my adversaries,
> > a horror to my neighbours,
> an object of dread to my acquaintances;
> > those who see me in the street flee from me.
> I have passed out of mind like one who is dead;
> > I have become like a broken vessel…
>
> Blessed be the Lord,
> > for he has wondrously shown his steadfast love to me
> > when I was beset as a city under siege.
> I had said in my alarm,
> > 'I am driven far from your sight.'
> But you heard my supplications
> > when I cried out to you for help.
> vv. 3–5, 9–12, 21–22

There is a wonderful BBC series called *The Repair Shop*, which never fails to move me to tears. In each episode someone brings along a broken item, often something with a family history which has been long discarded and forgotten. This is then lovingly restored by the team of brilliant craftspeople and returned to the family amid scenes of joy and amazement at the memories it then brings back.

The image of a discarded, broken vessel is one the psalmist uses to describe how he feels. He's scorned by his enemies, rejected by his neighbours, his body is failing, and things are so bad people run away from him in the street (vv. 10–12).

The psalm itself is rather like a broken pot, with each stanza being a shard of the whole biblical story, each telling a story of pain and redemption. The first verses remind us of David's time running from his murderous rival King Saul and of God as a 'rock' and a 'strong fortress' (v. 2), words that echo David's prayer in 2 Samuel 22:3. In verses 10–11 we are reminded of Job, who also felt that his bones were wasting away, and whose friends turned against him (Job 30). And we also recall Jesus, as it is this psalm that he goes to when uttering his final words on the cross: 'Into your hand I commit my spirit' (v. 5).

This is not a psalm of hopelessness and despair. The shards of brokenness are intertwined with prayer, praise and imagery of God's goodness and faithfulness. God the rock will lead his people to 'a broad place' (v. 8) and he has shown 'steadfast love' (v. 21) even amid pain and danger.

The Repair Shop can be seen as a deeply Christian programme, as it reminds us that everything and everyone matters and that there is nothing and no one so broken that they cannot be lovingly restored. We may feel at this time that we are of no value, that we have been broken beyond repair, spiritually, emotionally or physically. But that is not the case; there is hope that we too can be healed, made whole, repaired and restored. Jesus' broken and battered body was handed over to his Father, and three days later it was restored fully in the resurrection. That hope is for all of us, and the healing work can begin right now, but the full restoration work won't be complete until after mortal death. Music can be a way to begin any healing process and is especially helpful at times when we are most broken and bruised.

Further reading, reflection and prayer

Reading

O Lord, you are our Father;
we are the clay, and you are our potter;
we are all the work of your hand.
ISAIAH 64:8

Listen

The hymn 'It Is Well with My Soul' speaks to the hope of restoration, even after unimaginable loss and brokenness. Hymnodist Horatio Spafford wrote these beautiful words as he sailed across the Atlantic and passed near the spot where his four daughters had drowned in the 1873 sinking of the SS *Ville du Havre*. As Horatio travelled to meet his wife, who had survived the wreck, he penned these words, which have brought comfort to many over the years.

'It Is Well with My Soul' by Audrey Assad, *Inheritance* (2016)

Prayer

When peace like a river attendeth my way
When sorrows like sea billows roll
Whatever my lot, thou hast taught me to say
'It is well, it is well, with my soul'
Horatio Spafford (1828–88)

106

Psalm 38

'O my God, do not be far from me'

O Lord, do not rebuke me in your anger
    or discipline me in your wrath.
For your arrows have sunk into me,
    and your hand has come down on me.

There is no soundness in my flesh
    because of your indignation;
there is no health in my bones
    because of my sin.
For my iniquities have gone over my head;
    they weigh like a burden too heavy for me.

My wounds grow foul and fester
    because of my foolishness;
I am utterly bowed down and prostrate;
    all day long I go around mourning.

For my loins are filled with burning,
    and there is no soundness in my flesh.
I am utterly spent and crushed;
    I groan because of the tumult of my heart.

O Lord, all my longing is known to you;
    my sighing is not hidden from you.
My heart throbs; my strength fails me;
    as for the light of my eyes – it also has gone from me.
My friends and companions stand aloof from my affliction,
    and my neighbours stand far off…

But it is for you, O Lord, that I wait…

I confess my iniquity;
    I am sorry for my sin…

Do not forsake me, O Lord;
    O my God, do not be far from me;
make haste to help me,
    O Lord, my salvation.
vv. 1–11, 15, 18, 21–22

In my study I have a large copy of Rembrandt's *The Return of the Prodigal Son*. One of my favourite paintings, it depicts the moment the wayward son is welcomed back home into his father's expansive embrace after his time squandering his inheritance in 'dissolute living' (Luke 15:13). Luke's gospel describes the moment when the son realised he needed to turn back and return home as 'he came to his senses' (Luke 15:17).

There is a similar moment of realisation in the psalmist David's life. He had been so overwhelmed by lust for Bathsheba that he sent her husband, Uriah the Hittite, to the frontline of battle so that he would be killed and David would be free to marry her. The moment of realisation came when the prophet Nathan confronted him with the reality of what he had done ('You are the man!') and David comes to his senses and repents – 'I have sinned' (2 Samuel 12:7–15).

Psalm 38 is one of the seven penitential psalms, where the focus is on a person's awakening to their sin and need of God's love. We don't get to find out what has brought the psalmist here, but the impression is that it is serious and – whatever it is – has led them to a dark place. They are in physical (vv. 5, 7), mental (vv. 4, 6) and spiritual (v. 10) distress, and are socially ostracised (v. 12). But, unlike in so many other psalms, the cause isn't 'enemies' or some other external sources, but is personal: 'I am like one who does not hear' (v. 14); 'There is no health… because of my sin' (v. 3).

This is a person who is at rock bottom. They are 'utterly spent' (v. 8), which can also be translated as 'benumbed'. In *The Message* version of the Bible, it is translated as: 'I'm on my last legs; I've had it – my life is a vomit of groans.'

There is a misconception that we come to God by getting things right, by being good people and by never doing anything too terrible. However, the Bible shows us again and again that the way to God is not so linear. Rather, it's in realising we get it wrong time and again, coming to our senses and turning back to God – which is the meaning of repentance. The psalmist confesses 'I am sorry' and, like both David and the prodigal son, cries out, 'I confess my iniquity' (v. 18).

The miracle is that when we do that we are welcomed back into our Father's loving arms.

Further reading, reflection and prayer

Reading

So he set off and went to his father. But while he was still far off, his father saw him and was filled with compassion; he ran and put his arms around him and kissed him. Then the son said to him, 'Father, I have sinned against heaven and

before you; I am no longer worthy to be called your son.' But the father said to his slaves, 'Quickly, bring out a robe – the best one – and put it on him; put a ring on his finger and sandals on his feet. And get the fatted calf and kill it, and let us eat and celebrate, for this son of mine was dead and is alive again; he was lost and is found!' And they began to celebrate.
LUKE 15:20–24

Listen

'Prayer of St Gregory, Op. 62b' by Alan Hovhaness, Seattle Symphony Orchestra, *Symphony No. 2, 'Mysterious Mountain'/Prayer of St Gregory/And God Created Great Whales* (1994)

Prayer

Blessed Jesus, you are always near in times of stress.
Although we cannot feel your presence you are close.
You are always there to help and watch over us.
Nothing in heaven or on earth can separate us from you.
After Margery Kempe (c. 1373–1438)

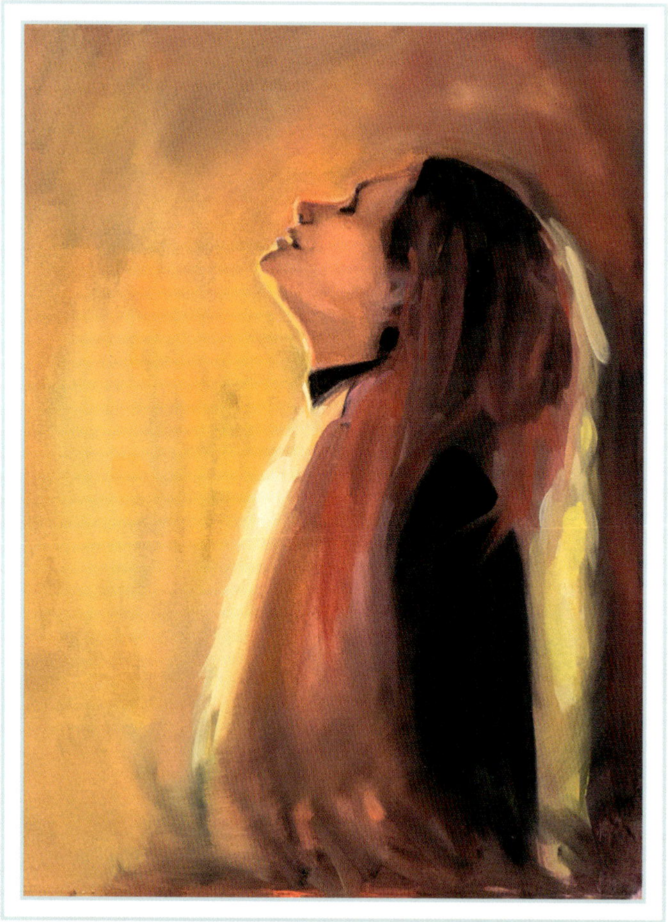

Psalm 39

'While I mused, the fire burned'

I said, 'I will guard my ways
   that I may not sin with my tongue;
I will keep a muzzle on my mouth
   as long as the wicked are in my presence.'
I was silent and still;
   I held my peace to no avail;
my distress grew worse;
   my heart became hot within me.
While I mused, the fire burned;
   then I spoke with my tongue:

'Lord, let me know my end
   and what is the measure of my days;
   let me know how fleeting my life is.
You have made my days a few handbreadths,

> and my lifetime is as nothing in your sight.
> Surely everyone stands as a mere breath. *Selah*
> > Surely everyone goes about like a shadow.
> Surely for nothing they are in turmoil;
> > they heap up and do not know who will gather.
>
> 'And now, O Lord, what do I wait for?
> > My hope is in you…
>
> 'For I am your passing guest,
> > an alien, like all my forebears.
> Turn your gaze away from me, that I may smile again,
> > before I depart and am no more.'
>
> vv. 1–7, 12–13

There are many psalms of complaint and lament, most ending with some glimmer of hope, where God hears the psalmist's cry, acts in some way, and well-being is restored. This is one of only two exceptions to that pattern (the other is Psalm 88). It's uncomfortable to read, as not only is there no resolution, but it ends with the writer hoping that God might turn away so they could be happy one last time before they die (v. 13). There is an honesty in this psalm that is refreshing, and many turn to psalms of lament in moments of hopelessness, as there is comfort in being able to express the reality of pain and anguish without sugar-coating it.

One of the greatest women of the 20th century was surely Mother Teresa of Calcutta, who spent her life among the most needy and vulnerable in India, winning the Nobel Peace Prize in 1979 for her work and canonised by the Catholic Church in 2016. After her death letters emerged which gave a rather surprising alternative view of her faith, where she confessed that she hadn't felt God's presence with her for over 50 years. She spoke of 'abandonment', 'dryness' and 'darkness', and at stages even doubted God's existence.

> In my soul I feel just that terrible pain of loss – of God not wanting me – of God not being God – of God not really existing (Jesus, please forgive my blasphemies…).[11]

This is a psalm for those who are struggling to find hope, and who have become fed up with pretending otherwise. The psalmist says he has kept quiet – 'a muzzle on my mouth' (v. 1) – but has 'held my peace to no avail' (v. 2). The frustration of keeping silent was like a spark that slowly grew until it burst out: 'While I mused, the fire burned; then I spoke' (v. 3).

The central question of this lament is: 'What is the purpose of life?' The psalmist concludes that it is but 'a mere breath', 'fleeting', a 'shadow', and at the end of it all we're just passing through, heaping up stuff for others to gather (vv. 4–6). There are echoes of Ecclesiastes here: 'I considered all that my hands had done and the toil I had spent in doing it, and again, all was vanity and a chasing after wind' (Ecclesiastes 2:11).

Despite all this, the psalmist still holds on to a glimmer of faith: 'Lord, what do I wait for? My hope is in you' (v. 7).

There is some irony in that many of Mother Teresa's letters expressing her feelings of disconnection from God, were in fact, written to God. In the very act of writing about not being able to pray, she was of course, praying.

The psalms remind us that we can say whatever we like to God; we don't need to pretend.

Further reading, reflection and prayer

Reading

> I hated all my toil in which I had toiled under the sun, seeing that I must leave it to my successor, and who knows whether will be wise or foolish? Yet he will be master of all for which I toiled and used my wisdom under the sun. This also is vanity. So I turned and gave my heart up to despair concerning all the toil of my labours under the sun…
>
> There is nothing better for mortals than to eat and drink and find enjoyment in their toil. This also, I saw, is from the hand of God, for apart from him who can eat or who can have enjoyment? For to the one who pleases him God gives wisdom and knowledge and joy.
> ECCLESIASTES 2:18–20, 24–26

Listen

'Concerto for Two Violins in D Minor, BWV 1043: II. Largo ma non tanto' by J.S. Bach, Andrew Manze, Rachel Podger, *Bach: Solo and Double Violin Concertos* (1997)

Prayer

Be present, O merciful God,
and protect us through the silent hours of the night,
so that we who are wearied by the changes and chances of this fleeting world
may repose upon thy eternal changelessness:
though Jesus Christ our Lord.

Gelasian Sacramentary

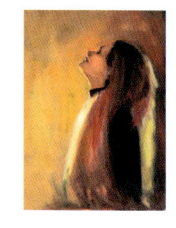

119

Psalm 57

'Awake, my soul!'

Be merciful to me, O God; be merciful to me,
>   for in you my soul takes refuge;
in the shadow of your wings I will take refuge,
>   until the destroying storms pass by.
I cry to God Most High,
>   to God who fulfils his purpose for me.
He will send from heaven and save me;
>   he will put to shame those who trample on me. *Selah*
God will send forth his steadfast love and his faithfulness.

I lie down among lions
>   that greedily devour human prey;
their teeth are spears and arrows,
>   their tongues sharp swords.

Be exalted, O God, above the heavens.
    Let your glory be over all the earth.

They set a net for my steps;
    my soul was bowed down.
They dug a pit in my path,
    but they have fallen into it themselves. *Selah*
My heart is steadfast, O God;
    my heart is steadfast.
I will sing and make melody.
    Awake, my soul!
Awake, O harp and lyre!
    I will awake the dawn.
I will give thanks to you, O Lord, among the peoples;
    I will sing praises to you among the nations.
For your steadfast love is as high as the heavens;
    your faithfulness extends to the clouds.

Be exalted, O God, above the heavens.
    Let your glory be over all the earth.

While we can't be sure of the author of every psalm, it is likely that this one, as the introduction to it suggests, is 'of David… when he fled from Saul, in the cave'. It's worth telling the story that is likely to have formed the context for this psalm.

David, the young shepherd boy who had been anointed by the prophet Samuel, had caught the eye of King Saul because of his ability to play the lyre, which calmed Saul's tormented soul. David became Saul's personal musician, then his armour bearer, and 'Saul loved him greatly' (1 Samuel 16:21). David was given a prominent place in the royal household, and eventually the hand of Saul's daughter Michal in marriage. However, Saul was a bitterly jealous man and as David began to grow in stature and prominence, particularly after seeing off the marauding rival Goliath with only his sling and a few stones, Saul became consumed with resentment. He became increasingly violent in his rages towards his young prodigy. David had to dodge spears, was sent to the frontline of battle and had to be protected from the king's rages by two of Saul's children, Jonathan and Michal. Saul's tempers eventually became so bad that David fled in the dead of night to a cave in the mountains.

The psalm speaks of a soul 'bowed down' (v. 6) and in need of protection: 'in the shadow of your wings I will take refuge' (v. 1). Perhaps it was in this cave that David uttered the prayer, 'Be merciful to me, O God; be merciful to me' (v. 1). If this is the case, then the psalmist's prayer was answered in an extraordinary way.

David remained in this cave for some time and developed a large following there as 'those who were with him numbered about four hundred' (1 Samuel 22:2). Saul wasn't going to give up easily and set off with his men to seek out his enemy. On the way he stumbled across David's cave and, without knowing his rival was inside, he used the cave as a toilet! While he 'went in to relieve himself', David snuck up behind him and snipped off a piece of his clothing. David immediately felt convicted by God, called off his men and spared Saul's life. The two rivals were reunited in a powerful and beautiful scene – David bowed down to Saul, recognising him as anointed by God; Saul 'lifted up his voice and wept' realising the error of his actions (1 Samuel 24).

We surely know what it is to be threatened or frightened to the point where we wish we could run away and hide. Similarly, we can perhaps recall times we've been so consumed by rage that we lose perspective and our souls become 'bowed down'.

The psalmist reminds us that God will be with us, even in the darkness of the deepest cave – in fact it is under God's protective wings that we are given refuge 'until the destroying storms pass by' (v. 1). And when the storms pass, which they surely will, how wonderful it will be to emerge from the cave into the glorious light, outstretch our arms in praise and to say:

> Awake, my soul! Awake, O harp and lyre! I will awake the dawn.
> v. 8

Further reading, reflection and prayer

Reading

> When David finished saying this, Saul asked, 'Is that your voice, David my son?' And he wept aloud. 'You are more righteous than I,' he said. 'You have treated me well, but I have treated you badly. You have just now told me about the good you did to me; the Lord gave me into your hands, but you did not kill me. When a man finds his enemy, does he let him get away unharmed? May the Lord reward you well for the way you treated me today. I know that you will surely be king and that the kingdom of Israel will be established in your hands.'
> 1 SAMUEL 24:16–20 (NIV)

Listen

The lyrics in this song seem like a cry of the heart from someone who longs for a spiritual awakening but often looks for this in the wrong places.

'Awake My Soul' by Mumford & Sons, *Sigh No More* (2009)

Prayer

O Lord, you are with us even in the darkest cave; protect us when our souls are bowed down, our hopes are crushed and all we want to do is hibernate. May we rest under the shadow of your wings until such a time that we can emerge from the gloom and raise our arms, and our souls can sing once again.

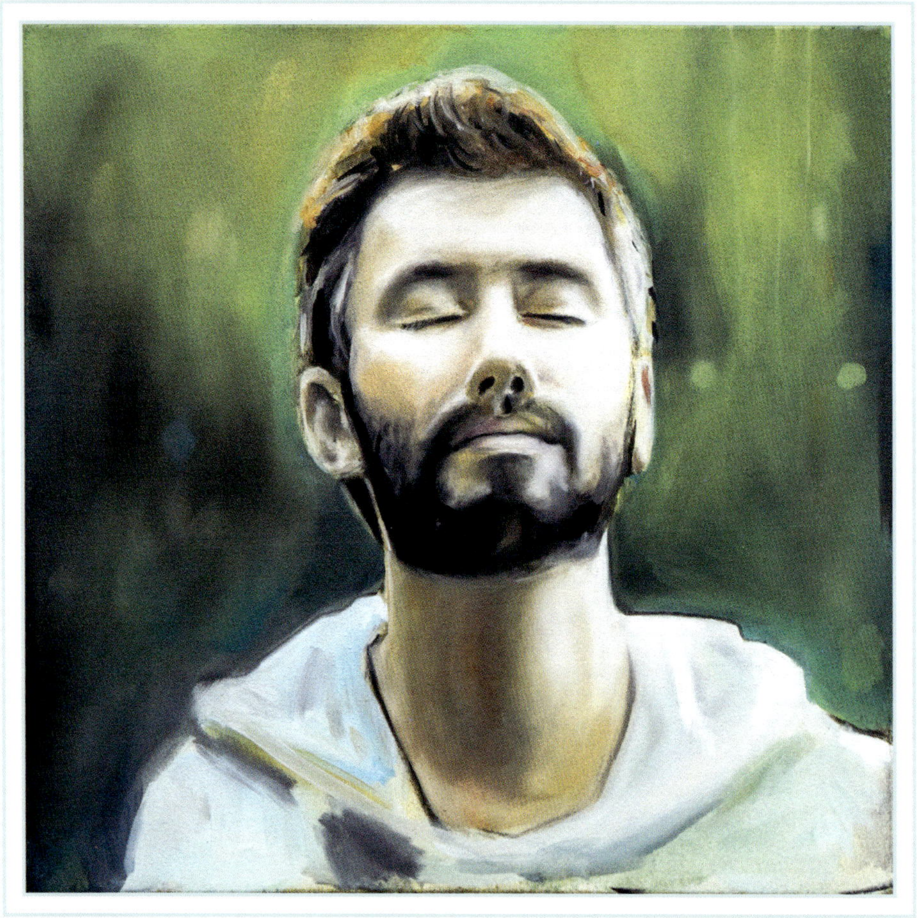

Psalm 62

'On God alone my soul in stillness waits'

For God alone my soul waits in silence;
from him comes my salvation.
He alone is my rock and my salvation,
my fortress; I shall never be shaken.

How long will you assail a person,
will you batter your victim, all of you,
as you would a leaning wall, a tottering fence?
Their only plan is to bring down a person of prominence.
They take pleasure in falsehood;
they bless with their mouths,
but inwardly they curse. *Selah*

For God alone my soul waits in silence,
> for my hope is from him.
He alone is my rock and my salvation,
> my fortress; I shall not be shaken.
On God rests my deliverance and my honour;
> my mighty rock, my refuge is in God.

Trust in him at all times, O people;
> pour out your heart before him;
> God is a refuge for us. *Selah*

Those of low estate are but a breath;
> those of high estate are a delusion;
in the balances they go up;
> they are together lighter than a breath…

Once God has spoken;
> twice have I heard this:
that power belongs to God,
> and steadfast love belongs to you, O Lord.
For you repay to all
> according to their work.

vv. 1–9, 11–12

My preferred translation of verse 1 of this psalm comes from the Common Worship Psalter and is, in my view, one of the most beautiful lines of scripture:

> On God alone my soul in stillness waits.

It deserves repeating over again in the stillness of wherever you are right now.

There are remarkably few examples of silent prayer in scripture; most prayer is communal, spoken out loud and/or accompanied by instruments. The psalms present us a range of different ways in which we can communicate with God, most of which are rather noisy, involving crying out in distress, pleading for mercy or praising with harps and lyres.

Here we have an example of prayer in stillness and solitude.

The psalmist has been through times of unrest and instability; the imagery is powerful, that of 'a leaning wall, a tottering fence' (v. 3), which imbues a sense of vulnerability, as if the person's very boundaries have been eroded. The repetition of 'I shall never be shaken' (vv. 2, 6) makes us think that perhaps they have indeed felt on unstable ground in some way. In contrast, God is 'my rock', 'my fortress' and 'my salvation' (vv. 2, 6–7).

It's in these times of instability and uncertainty that we might be best advised to take some time in stillness and solitude. One of the disciplines of being a priest is to take regular retreats, and as a consummate extrovert I've always had a love–hate relationship with the silent versions. The enforced silence before being ordained deacon was a low point, mainly because it was a time of heightened anxiety and the retreat leader scowled if we so much as looked at another ordinand and insisted on playing smooth classics over breakfast, which just made us snigger. However, I've come to yearn for the space to get away from the relentlessness of the noise of our modern-day world and relish the few days of peace a silent retreat offers.

My most powerful retreat experience was after a long and difficult conflict in my work situation, and I went on silent retreat to Bueno's, a Jesuit retreat centre in north Wales. As I sat in silence with the turmoil of my past experiences buzzing round my head I noticed the altar in the chapel. The altar table was made up of a large slab of thin stone which seemed to be teetering on a pile of boulders stacked into a point. At first, I had a strong desire to pick one of the rocks and throw it – I was angry at the time! But as I sat there, doing nothing but waiting, a powerful sense of peace came over me and I knew, deep in my soul, that it would be alright. For me, that altar represented the fragility and vulnerability of my life and faith in contrast to the permanence and solidness of God's love, and that was enough.

The psalm ends with words of comfort:

> Power belongs to God,
> and steadfast love belongs to you, O Lord.
> vv. 11–12

It may not always be possible to go away on retreat, but it is often possible to find little pockets of retreat within our daily lives, even if that's just taking a few moments alone on a walk or even in the bath! This psalm invites us to stop, pause and rest in God for a while, perhaps repeating that beautiful first verse:

> On God alone my soul in stillness waits.

Further reading, reflection and prayer

Reading

> 'Go out and stand on the mountain before the Lord, for the Lord is about to pass by.' Now there was a great wind, so strong that it was splitting mountains and breaking rocks in pieces before the Lord, but the Lord was not in the wind, and after the wind an earthquake, but the Lord was not in the earthquake, and after the earthquake a fire, but the Lord was not in the fire, and after the fire a sound of sheer silence.
> 1 KINGS 19:11–12

Listen

'Be Still, My Soul' by Libera, *Angel Voices* (2006)

Prayer

Alone with none but thee, my God,
I journey on my way.
What need I fear when thou art near,
O King of night and day?
More safe am I within thy hand
Than if an host didst round me stand.

Attributed to St Columba (c. 521–597)

134

Psalm 64

'Surely the human mind and heart are cunning'

Hear me, my God, as I voice my complaint;
protect my life from the threat of the enemy.

Hide me from the conspiracy of the wicked,
    from the plots of evildoers.
They sharpen their their tongues like swords
    and aim cruel words like deadly arrows.
They shoot from ambush at the innocent;
    they shoot suddenly, without fear.

They encourage each other in evil plans,
    they talk about hiding their snares;
    they say, 'Who will see it?'

They plot injustice and say,
    'We have devised a perfect plan!'
    Surely the human mind and heart are cunning.

But God will shoot them with his arrows;
    they will suddenly be struck down.
He will turn their own tongues against them
    and bring them to ruin;
    all who see them will shake their heads in scorn.
All people will fear;
    they will proclaim the works of God
    and ponder what he has done.

The righteous will rejoice in the Lord
    and take refuge in him;
    all the upright in heart will glory in him!
(NIV)

I have a confession. One of the ways I like to relax is to listen to true crime podcasts. I don't like anything particularly gory or the ones that focus on the violent death of women, but I do enjoy the excellent storytelling and clever detective work that so often come with this genre. The most satisfying ones will involve a miscarriage of justice, a perpetrator who is convinced their story is watertight and they've got away with it, and then a shift as mistakes are made, holes in the story appear and justice is eventually served. They can be enormously satisfying, if a little gruesome at times.

There is a similar sense of injustice and threat throughout this psalm, as in some true crime podcasts. I imagine it will resonate with anyone who has been on the sharp end of any dispute or legal battle. There are 'enemies', 'threats', 'secret plots' and 'evil plans'. The fear isn't of physical warfare in this psalm, but rather a more insidious violence which is dealt by words which cut like swords and cruel comments which sting like sharp arrows.

The evil here is hidden from public view, and this is what is so threatening. It is an evil that's not obvious to the outside world – 'No one can see us. We'll commit a perfect crime,' they say. As I read this psalm, I thought of the woman I know who was subjected to years of coercive control from her partner, and of my friend who was stalked online by a bitter former colleague. They have both spoken to me of the fear of not knowing what's coming next and of the exhaustion of trying to work out the psyche of their harasser so they can try to predict their behaviour. As the psalmist puts it, 'The human heart and mind are cunning' (v. 6, NIV), or as *The Message* puts it, 'The Detective detects the mystery in the dark of the cellar heart.'

There is a pivotal moment in the middle of the psalm, where the power shifts away from the perpetrator and God intervenes and strikes back:

> But God will shoot his arrow at them;
> they will be wounded suddenly.
> v. 7

It is a reminder that in the end all those who harm us and who do wrong will have to face divine judgement, even if this doesn't end up happening in their lifetime. I find this a liberating thought. The apostle Paul in his letter to the Romans describes how a 'true Christian' might behave towards those who persecute them; it's a challenging text, which ends: 'Never avenge yourselves, but leave room for the wrath of God' (Romans 12:19).

In the meantime, we can take comfort in the protection of God that the psalmist prays for at the beginning and which is provided at the end: 'Let the righteous rejoice in the Lord and take refuge in him' (v. 10).

Further reading, reflection and prayer

Reading

Rejoice with those who rejoice; weep with those who weep. Live in harmony with one another… If it is possible… live peaceably with all.
ROMANS 12:15–16, 18

Listen

'Adagio (Albinoni)' by Angèle Dubeau, Rachèle Laurin, *Immortalis: A journey into the world of sacred and secular music* (2006)

Prayer

I [pray] also for all those whom I have in any way grieved, vexed, oppressed and scandalised, by word or deed, knowingly or unknowingly; that thou mayest equally forgive us all our sins, and all our offences against each other.
Thomas à Kempis (1380—1471)

Psalms of joy

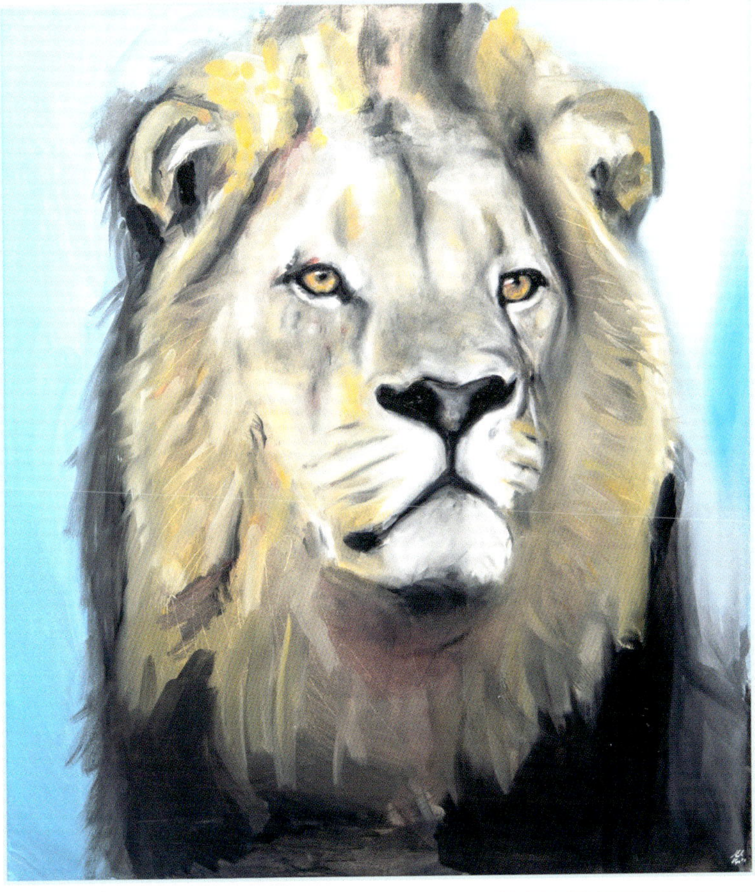

Psalm 2

'Therefore, O kings, be wise'

Why do the nations conspire,
    and the peoples plot in vain?
The kings of the earth set themselves,
    and the rulers take counsel together,
    against the Lord and his anointed, saying,
'Let us burst their bonds apart
    and cast their cords from us.'

He who sits in the heavens laughs;
    the Lord has them in derision.
Then he will speak to them in his wrath
    and terrify them in his fury, saying,
'I have set my king on Zion, my holy hill.'

I will tell of the decree of the Lord:
He said to me, 'You are my son;
    today I have begotten you.
Ask of me, and I will make the nations your heritage
    and the ends of the earth your possession.
You shall break them with a rod of iron
    and dash them in pieces like a potter's vessel.'

Now therefore, O kings, be wise;
    be warned, O rulers of the earth.
Serve the Lord with fear,
    with trembling kiss his feet,
or he will be angry, and you will perish in the way,
    for his wrath is quickly kindled.

Happy are all who take refuge in him.

The Emperor Diocletian ruled the Roman Empire from AD284–305 and spent much of it persecuting the early church and attempting to eradicate Christianity. He razed churches, burned scriptures, executed believers and prohibited gatherings. His Great Persecution of AD303 was brutal, and at the height of his rule he set up a monument on the Spanish frontier of his empire with the inscription:

> Diocletian Jovian Maximian Herculeus Caesares Augusti for having extended the Roman Empire in the east and the west and for having extinguished the name of Christians who brought the republic to ruin.[12]

Of course, his plan failed and followers of Jesus now make up the largest faith group in the world, numbering over two billion.

Religious persecution is as old as faith itself, and this psalm seems to be set within the context of an attack on Judea by an alliance of nations who were seeking, once again, to subjugate the Jewish people (v. 3). I am writing this while conflicts in Ukraine, Myanmar, the Middle East and Sudan (to name just a few) are raging and where the seemingly intractable political, geographical and religious issues have led to the deaths of many thousands of innocent people. The psalmist asks, 'Why do the nations so furiously rage?' (as translated in Handel's *Messiah*), a question we no doubt all continue to ask ourselves!

This is a psalm about the hubris of those who rule the nations, thinking they are invincible and can evade God's judgement. The psalm puts human power into an eternal perspective. God 'laughs', holds them 'in derision', will 'terrify them in his fury' and 'speak to them in his wrath' (vv. 4–5). It's not an easy read for those in a position of authority!

While Psalm 1 (which I recommend you read as well) is about God's promise to individual people, this psalm is about God's promises to a nation. The king in verse 6 is likely to be David, the shepherd boy anointed as king of an eternal dynasty, as prophesied by the prophet Nathan:

> [David] is the one who will build a house for my Name, and I will establish the throne of his kingdom forever. I will be his father, and he shall be my son. When he does wrong, I will punish him… But my love will never be taken away from him.
> 2 SAMUEL 7:13–15 (NIV)

This promise forms the bedrock of Israel's hope for a messiah, and Christians believe this promise was fulfilled in the person of Jesus, a very different kind of king, one who was born from David's line but who brought into being a kingdom based on humility, service and love, and who wore a rather different kind of crown as he died.

When we consider a world where people are still being persecuted for their faith, where conflicts continue to rage and where leaders still believe themselves to be above reproach, perhaps this psalm can be a comfort – there will one day be judgement:

> Therefore, O kings, be wise;
>   be warned, O rulers of the earth.
>
> v. 10

Further reading, reflection and prayer

Reading

> And now, O Lord my God, you have made your servant king in place of my father David, although I am only a little child; I do not know how to go out or come in. And your servant is in the midst of the people whom you have chosen, a great people so numerous they cannot be numbered or counted. Give your servant, therefore, an understanding mind to govern your people, able to discern between good and evil, for who can govern this your great people of yours?'
>
> 1 KINGS 3:7–9

Listen

'Why Do the Nations So Furiously Rage Together' by The Tabernacle Choir at Temple Square, Orchestra at Temple Square, *Handel's Messiah* (2016)

Prayer

Eternal Light, shine into our hearts,
Eternal Goodness, deliver us from evil,
Eternal Power, be our support,
Eternal Wisdom, scatter the darkness of our ignorance,
Eternal Pity, have mercy on us;
that with all our heart and mind and strength
we may seek thy face and be brought by thine infinite mercy
to thy holy presence; through Jesus Christ our Lord.
Alcuin of York (c. 735–804)

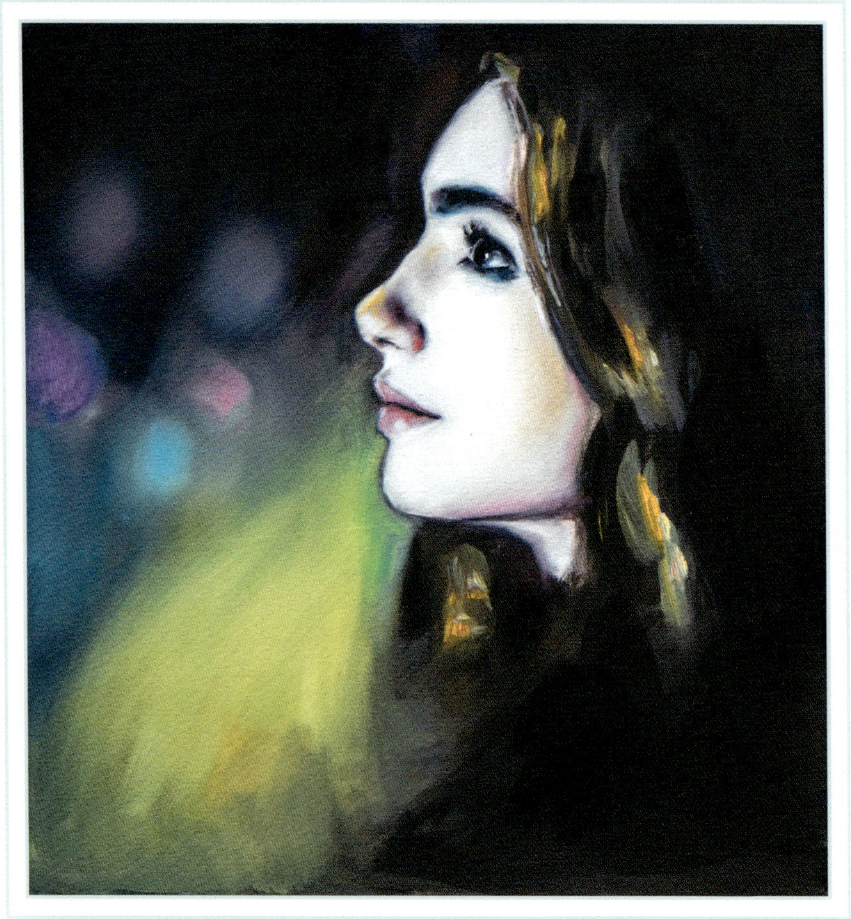

Psalm 27

'Behold the beauty of the Lord'

The Lord is my light and my salvation;
   whom shall I fear?
The Lord is the stronghold of my life;
   of whom shall I be afraid?…

Though an army encamp against me,
   my heart shall not fear;
though war rise up against me,
   yet I will be confident.

One thing I asked of the Lord,
   this I seek:
to live in the house of the Lord
   all the days of my life,

to behold the beauty of the Lord,
    and to inquire in his temple.

For he will hide me in his shelter
    in the day of trouble;
he will conceal me under the cover of his tent;
    he will set me high on a rock.

Now my head is lifted up
    above my enemies all around me,
and I will offer in his tent
    sacrifices with shouts of joy;
I will sing and make melody to the Lord.

Hear, O Lord, when I cry aloud;
    be gracious to me and answer me!
'Come,' my heart says, 'seek his face!'
    Your face, Lord, do I seek.
    Do not hide your face from me.

vv. 1, 3–9

What is so comforting and reassuring in the Psalms is that they allow for the whole gamut of human emotion, not just psalm by psalm, but so often all muddled together in one psalm, much the way we find in life. Psalm 27 is one you could spend a year pondering and still find different images and emotions to dwell on.

One of the things I'm most afraid of is heights. As a mother of three sons, I've always enjoyed joining them on outdoor challenges, never wanting to be the kind of parent that sits on the sidelines. This was all fine until the time I became stranded on one of those tree-top high ropes and had to be rescued by the guide and brought down. I remember standing on the small board at the top of a tree, clutching the bark with my heart beating and my body refusing to move. I knew deep down that I was strapped in, that the ropes would hold me and that I was safe, but at the very same time I was terrified. The only thing that kept me from panicking was singing the hymn 'Dear Lord and Father of mankind' until help came!

Although it's titled a 'triumphant song of confidence', there is a sense of fear pervading this psalm. The psalmist is beset by evildoers, adversaries and foes (v. 2), and there is a feeling of abandonment by God (v. 9) and by family (v. 10), both of whom they'd expected to be there for protection. Despite this, it is a psalm of courage – courage in the face of adversity. You can imagine David speaking it line by line as he and his men flee from King Saul and are hunted down.

This psalm allows for complexity, for paradox. We can know deep down that we are safe, that we are loved or that we belong, but at the very same time feel unsafe, unloved or alone. And conversely, we can deep down feel threatened, fearful and abandoned while at the same time knowing that we are never abandoned by a God who loves us.

I am reminded of two instances in the gospels. First, of the father of the boy with seizures, who pleads for Jesus to heal his son when he says: 'I believe; help my unbelief!' (Mark 9:24). And second, of the disciples after witnessing the bodily resurrection of Jesus, who 'yet for all their joy were still were disbelieving and wondering' (Luke 24:41).

In a similar way, in contrast to the psalm's pervading sense of fear, the final verse strikes a note of courage:

> Wait for the Lord;
>> be strong, and let your heart take courage;
>> wait for the Lord!
>
> v. 14

The root of the word 'courage' is *cor*, the Latin for heart. In one of its earliest forms, the word courage meant 'to speak one's mind by telling one's heart'.[13]

'BEHOLD THE BEAUTY OF THE LORD' 153

In the midst of the turmoil of life, and at those times when we are feeling most threatened, fearful and vulnerable, the invitation of this psalm is to embrace such turmoil and emotions rather than running away from them. Sometimes all that means is taking time to 'behold' the beauty all around us (v. 4), to 'wait for the Lord' (v. 14) and to sing God's praises, even when we're afraid (v. 6).

Further reading, reflection and prayer

Reading

> Do not be anxious about anything, but in everything by prayer and supplication with thanksgiving let your requests be made known to God. And the peace of God, which surpasses all understanding, will guard your hearts and your minds in Christ Jesus.
> PHILIPPIANS 4:6–7

Listen

'Concerto in C Major for Sopranino Recorder, Strings and BC, RV 443: II. Largo' by by Karl Strangenberg, Munich Chamber Orchestra and Hans Stadlmeier, *Baroque Concertos for Recorder* (2009)

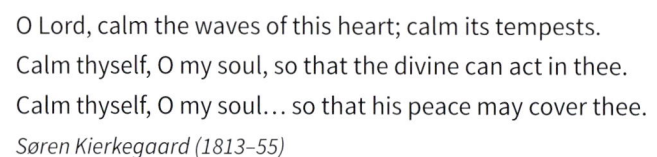

Prayer

O Lord, calm the waves of this heart; calm its tempests.
Calm thyself, O my soul, so that the divine can act in thee.
Calm thyself, O my soul… so that his peace may cover thee.
Søren Kierkegaard (1813–55)

155

Psalm 49

'People, despite their wealth, do not endure'

Hear this, all you peoples;
  listen, all who live in this world,
both low and high,
   rich and poor alike:
My mouth will speak words of wisdom;
   the meditation of my heart will give you understanding.
I will turn my ear to a proverb;
   with the harp I will expound my riddle:

Why should I fear when evil days come,
   when wicked deceivers surround me –
those who trust in their wealth
   and boast of their great riches?

No one can redeem the life of another
    or give to God a ransom for them…
For all can see that the wise die,
    that the foolish and the senseless also perish,
    leaving their wealth to others.
Their tombs will remain their houses forever,
    their dwellings for endless generations,
    though they had named lands after themselves.

People, despite their wealth, do not endure;
    they are like the beasts that perish…

But God will redeem me from the realm of the dead;
    he will surely take me to himself.
Do not be overawed when others grow rich,
    when the splendour of their houses increases;
for they will take nothing with them when they die,
    their splendour will not descend with them.
vv. 1–7, 10–12, 15–17 (NIV)

In my 20s I travelled to China with a couple of friends and visited the incredible terracotta army in Xian. There were rows upon rows of clay soldiers, 8,000 of them in total, all built with the intention of protecting the first emperor, Qin Shi Huang (born around 259BC) in his afterlife. It is said that he was so obsessed with eternal life that he would consume mercury sulphide, a poisonous solution that no doubt did the opposite and took him to an early grave.

The obsession with riches and immortality is nothing new. Stephen Cave, in his book *Immortality* describes this fascination as being hardwired into human experience, but as essentially futile. He writes 'Life is a constant war we are doomed to lose' and 'Death is meticulous in collecting every living thing sooner or later.'[14]

The psalmist is making a similar point in this wisdom song. It is a clarion call to humankind, 'Hear this, all you peoples' (v. 1), to wake up to the fact that all the wealth, power and riches we accumulate will make no difference in the end. It's impossible to make any kind of bargain with God to escape this stark fact (v. 7). Emperor Huang couldn't wager with the grim reaper, and neither can the rest of us.

> For all can see that the wise die,
>   that the foolish and the senseless also perish,
>   leaving their wealth to others.
> v. 10 (NIV)

It's perhaps not the cheeriest of psalms, but then truth sometimes stings a little. It reminds me of the poem by Percy Shelley about a traveller in the desert encountering a pedestal with an inscription:

> My name is Ozymandias, King of Kings;
> Look on my works, ye Mighty, and despair!
> Nothing beside remains. Round the decay
> Of that colossal wreck, boundless and bare
> The lone and level sands stretch far away.[15]

So, if we can't take anything with us, and if even the memory of us will no doubt fade before too long, what is there to hope for?

Jesus met a rich man on his travels who was also asking questions about eternal life (Mark 10:17), and Jesus challenged him to give up what he had to sell to those in need 'and you will have treasure in heaven' (Mark 10:21). Sadly for him this was too much to ask for and he went away grieving. For us, though, seeking treasure in heaven rather than treasure on earth is surely more likely to lead to life in all its fullness. The way to do this is to focus more on our relationship with God than the number of things we accumulate during our lifetime.

Further reading, reflection and prayer

Reading

'Do not store up for yourselves treasures on earth, where moths and vermin destroy, and where thieves break in and steal. But store up for yourselves treasures in heaven, where moths and vermin do not destroy, and where thieves do not break in and steal. For where your treasure is, there your heart will be also.'
MATTHEW 6:19–21 (NIV)

Listen

'Psalm 49 – O Hear Ye This, All Ye People' by The Choir of St John's College, Cambridge, *Psalms of Consolation and Hope* (1978)

Prayer

Take from us, O God, all pride and vanity, all boasting and forwardness, and give us the true courage that shows itself by gentleness; the true wisdom that shows itself by simplicity; and the true power that shows itself by modesty; through Jesus Christ our Lord.

Charles Kingsley (1819–75)

162

Psalm 71

'Do not cast me off in the time of old age'

In you, O Lord, I take refuge;
let me never be put to shame.
In your righteousness deliver me and rescue me;
incline your ear to me and save me.
Be to me a rock of refuge,
a strong fortress to save me,
for you are my rock and my fortress.

Rescue me, O my God, from the hand of the wicked,
from the grasp of the unjust and cruel.
For you, O Lord, are my hope,
my trust, O Lord, from my youth.
From my birth I have leaned upon you,

my protector since my mother's womb.
My praise is continually of you...

Do not cast me off in the time of old age;
   do not forsake me when my strength is spent...

But I will hope continually
   and will praise you yet more and more.
My mouth will tell of your righteous acts,
   of your deeds of salvation all day long,
   though their number is past my knowledge.
I will come praising the mighty deeds of the Lord God,
   I will praise your righteousness, yours alone;

O God, from my youth you have taught me,
   and I still proclaim your wondrous deeds.
So even to old age and grey hairs,
   O God, do not forsake me,
until I proclaim your might
   to all the generations to come.
Your power and your righteousness, O God,
   reach the high heavens.

> You who have done great things,
>   O God, who is like you?
> vv. 1–6, 9, 14–19

We hear Michael a minute before he arrives at our student chapel service, as he uses a stick and it clicks loudly on the stone floor of the cathedral as he slowly makes his way to the Lady Chapel for our weekly service of College Communion. He is in his late 80s and comes along faithfully every week. Over breakfast afterwards the students love hearing his stories of his time at the college as a young man and about his fascinating tales, which meander from ladybirds (an area in which he is an expert) to the classics and French poetry. He often tells the story of being utterly devastated when he was turned down for a PhD, but this propelled him into teaching, which, alongside his family, was the great love of his life. I find it immensely moving to watch how he passes on nuggets of wisdom to my college students while he simultaneously benefits from being listened to and takes great joy in being surrounded by bright young things.

Psalm 71 is a psalm for those who are getting on in years and who feel they might be past their prime. 'Do not cast me off in the time of old age,' the psalmist cries, 'do not forsake me when my strength is spent' (v. 9). Our culture is horribly focused on youth, and so many elderly people do feel 'cast off' and set aside when their perceived usefulness has waned. Loneliness is a particular problem for elderly people. According to Age UK, more than 2 million people in England over the age of 75 live alone, and more than a million older people say they go over a month without speaking to a friend, neighbour or family member.[16] I can't imagine not talking to someone for a day let alone a month!

The psalmist is an old man whose life isn't easy. He is still experiencing injustice and cruelty (v. 4) and is in need of God's strength and protection (vv. 1–2). But despite this he is reflecting on and remembering all the times he has been faithful to God: 'My trust, O Lord, from my youth' (v. 5); 'O God, from my youth you have taught me' (v. 17). As he remembers this, he also recalls all the times that God has been faithful to him: 'You are my rock and my fortress' (v. 3).

There are many examples in the Bible where God uses older people to bring about his purposes, such as the priest Eli, who teaches the young prophet Samuel to listen (1 Samuel 3), and Simeon and Anna, who recognise the infant Jesus as the Messiah (Luke 2:22–38). In fact, the elderly prophet Anna is the inspiration for the wonderful work of BRF Ministries' Anna Chaplaincy which supports the spiritual care of older people.[17]

One of the great benefits of growing older is that you get to have a longer perspective, so the things that once seemed to be the greatest disaster (like Michael not getting accepted on that PhD course) turn out to lead to other blessings. In God's eyes we are never 'cast aside' or useless. Our value isn't based on productivity, income or status but rather on being a member of the family of God. Hopefully whatever age we are we can say:

> You who have done great things,
> O God, who is like you?
> v. 19

Further reading, reflection and prayer

Reading

> There was also a prophet, Anna the daughter of Phanuel, of the tribe of Asher. She was of a great age, having lived with her husband for seven years after her marriage, then as a widow to the age of eighty-four. She never left the temple but worshipped there with fasting and prayer night and day. At that moment she came and began to praise God and to speak about the child to all who were looking for the redemption of Jerusalem.
> LUKE 2:36–38

Listen

'Hamabdil for cello and harp (Hebrew melody)' by Granville Bantock, Sandrine Chatron, Ophélie Gaillard, *A British Promenade* (2017)

This piece of music was inspired by a Jewish hymn normally sung at the conclusion of the Sabbath service.

Prayer

Faithful God, you have promised in Christ to be with us to the end of time. Come close to those who have lived long and experienced much. Help them to continue to be faithful and, within the all-age kingdom of God, to find ways to go on giving and receiving your grace, day by day. For your glory and your kingdom. Amen.
The Anna Chaplaincy Prayer

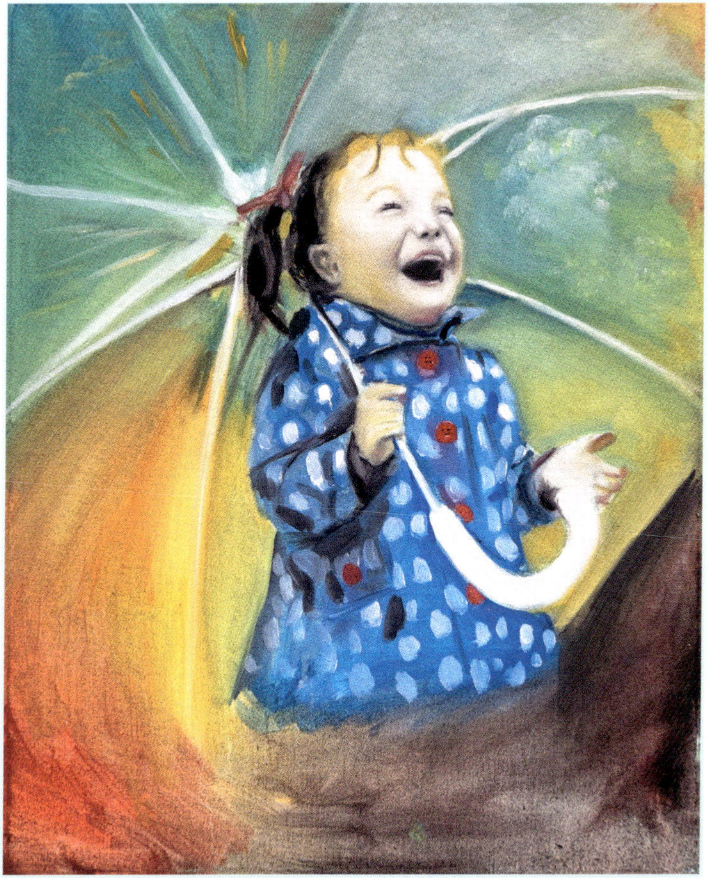

Psalm 72

'May he be like rain'

Give the king your justice, O God,
    and your righteousness to a king's son.
May he judge your people with righteousness
    and your poor with justice.
May the mountains yield prosperity for the people,
    and the hills, in righteousness.
May he defend the cause of the poor of the people,
    give deliverance to the needy,
    and crush the oppressor…

May he be like rain that falls on the mown grass,
    like showers that water the earth.
In his days may righteousness flourish
    and peace abound, until the moon is no more…

For he delivers the needy when they call,
>   the poor and those who have no helper.
> He has pity on the weak and the needy
>   and saves the lives of the needy…

May there be abundance of grain in the land;
>   may it wave on the tops of the mountains;
>   may its fruit be like Lebanon;
> and may people blossom in the cities
>   like the grass of the field.
> May his name endure forever,
>   his fame continue as long as the sun.
> May all nations be blessed in him;
>   may they pronounce him happy.

Blessed be the Lord, the God of Israel,
>   who alone does wondrous things.
>
> vv. 1–4, 6–7, 12–13, 16–18

King Charles III was crowned on 6 May 2023 in Westminster Abbey in an opulent and magnificent ceremony involving oaths, the anointing with holy oil and prayers for his reign. As he was anointed the choir sang the anthem 'Zadok the Priest' by Handel, as it has been at every coronation since George II in 1727. The anthem marks the moment that Solomon was anointed at the end of his father King David's reign:

> Zadok the priest and Nathan the prophet anointed Solomon king.
> And all the people rejoiced and said:
> God save the King! Long live the King! God save the King!
> May the King live forever. Amen. Hallelujah.

Solomon was not the most likely heir to David's throne, as he had several older brothers, including Adonijah, who also declared himself king. Solomon's mother Bathsheba and the prophet Nathan advocated Solomon as successor, and David saw to it that he would be anointed as king.

Psalm 72 begins 'Of Solomon', indicating that it was written as a prayer for his reign. It is a beautiful example of what good governance might look like and what we might pray for in a national leader. The psalm is one of hope and yearning for a nation and, unlike so many others, it is peaceful throughout and doesn't mention military might or power, except for one glancing mention of 'foes' bowing down before him (v. 9). The psalmist prays that the reign would be one of justice, righteousness and deliverance, where the king would 'defend the cause of the poor' (v. 4) and have 'pity on the weak and the needy' (v. 13) and where peace would 'abound' (v. 7).

The language uses the metaphor of the production of the land as an expression of God's faithfulness and the king's good governance:

> May he be like rain that falls on the mown grass,
> like showers that water the earth.
> v. 6

> May people blossom…
> like the grass of the field.
> v. 16

Did King Solomon live up to the aspirations of this prayer? He was known for his wisdom and good judgement and his reign was one of prosperity and largely peaceful. However, rather than focus on the poor, the needy and the oppressed, King Solomon accrued vast wealth for himself and had a thousand wives and concubines! His numerous wives brought the worship of foreign gods into the temple and 'turned away his heart' from God (1 Kings 11:3), and this descent into idolatry angered God and led to the separation of the kingdom after his death.

No earthly ruler will ever live up to the aspirations in this psalm in its entirety, but perhaps it can help us in our prayers for leaders and those with authority in our nations. We can pray that they would lead with integrity, justice and peace and that they would put the needs of the poor and needy at the forefront of their policies. Ultimately, we look towards Jesus, who is the true 'king of kings', whose rule is one of true justice and whose 'name [will] endure forever' (v. 17).

Further reading, reflection and prayer

Reading

> When David's time to die drew near, he charged his son Solomon… 'I am about to go the way of all the earth. Be strong, be courageous, and keep the charge of the Lord your God, walking in his ways and keeping his statutes, his commandments, his ordinances, and his testimonies… so that you may prosper in all that you do.'
> 1 KINGS 2:1–3

Listen

'Zadok the Priest' by The Choir of Westminster Abbey, *Handel: Die Schönsten Chöre* (2009)

Prayer

Father of all mankind, we pray thee to turn to thyself the hearts of all peoples and their rulers, that by the power of the Holy Spirit peace may be established on the foundation of justice, righteousness, and truth; through him who was lifted up on the cross to draw all men to himself, even thy Son Jesus Christ.

William Temple (1881–1944)

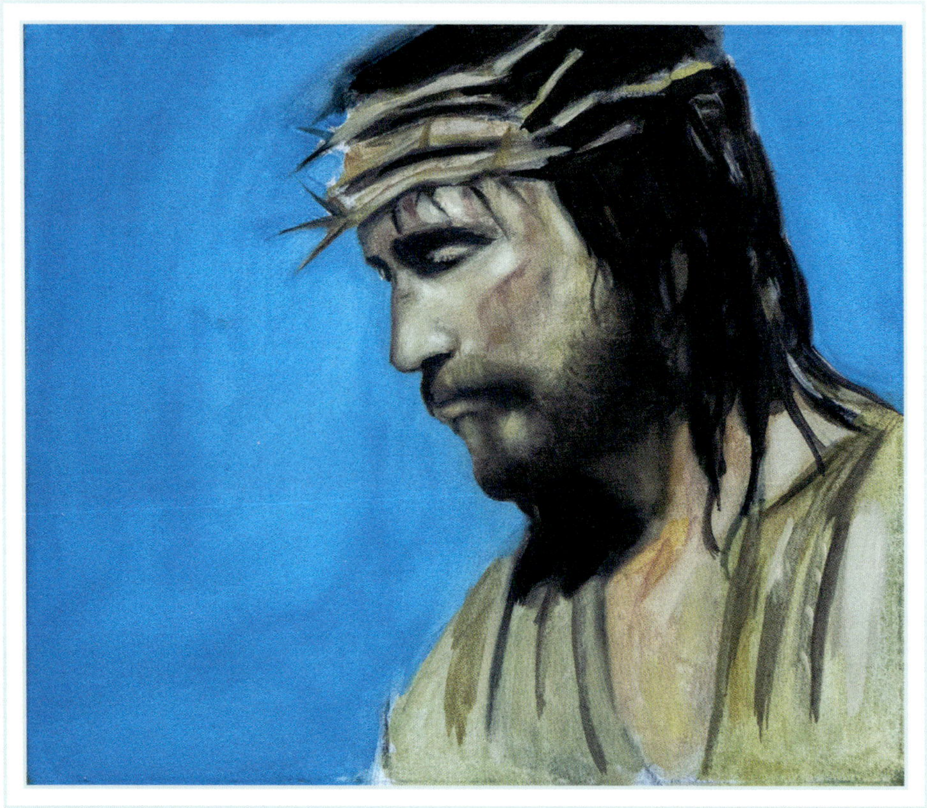

Psalm 81

'I relieved your shoulder of the burden'

I relieved your shoulder of the burden;
  your hands were freed from the basket.
In distress you called, and I rescued you;
  I answered you in the secret place of thunder;
  I tested you at the waters of Meribah. *Selah*
Hear, O my people, while I admonish you;
  O Israel, if you would but listen to me!
There shall be no strange god among you;
  you shall not bow down to a foreign god.
I am the Lord your God,
  who brought you up out of the land of Egypt.
  Open your mouth wide, and I will fill it.

'But my people did not listen to my voice;
  Israel would not submit to me.

> So I gave them over to their stubborn hearts,
>   to follow their own counsels.
> O that my people would listen to me,
>   that Israel would walk in my ways!
> Then I would quickly subdue their enemies
>   and turn my hand against their foes.
> Those who hate the Lord would cringe before him,
>   and their doom would last forever.
> I would feed you with the finest of the wheat,
>   and with honey from the rock I would satisfy you.'
> vv. 6–16

I remember when my three boys were young, I would often get to the stage where I was speaking to them but they, purposely or not, just didn't seem to hear a single thing I was saying. It was immensely frustrating, and I remember once standing on a chair and shouting in frustration at being ignored: 'Will you just listen to me!'

The psalm begins with a lot of noise: there are songs, trumpets, tambourines and shouts for joy (vv. 1–5). It's a celebration, and the reference to the moon makes it likely that this is referring to the Jewish festival of Sukkot, a seven-day festival which commemorates the exodus from Egypt and God's provision of sustenance for the

Israelites. The psalm refers to this period of Jewish history with a reminder that 'I relieved your shoulder of the burden… I rescued you; I answered you' (vv. 6–7).

But the central point of this psalm is a sense of deep frustration that, despite God's faithfulness and the clear evidence of his provision, the people refused to listen (vv. 8, 11, 13) and, even worse, turned away to other gods (v. 9) and followed their own ideas (v. 12). It refers to Meribah, which is the place of conflict between Moses and the newly freed Israelites (Exodus 17:7). Almost as soon as they had been released from captivity, making their miraculous escape across the Red Sea, the Israelites began to grumble and complain. They first moaned about the lack of food, and God sent them manna and quail (Exodus 16). Soon after they complained to Moses that they didn't have enough water to drink. And Moses, at the Lord's command, took a staff and struck a rock, which then produced the water which sustained them. They grumbled again soon after.

We often consider the unconditional love of God, and there are plenty of examples of this in scripture (John's gospel is full of them). But it is also true that in the Bible God's love is conditional as well, as there are certain expectations which flow from that love. Richard Rohr writes that 'any law, correction, rule or limitation is another word for conditional love', and he explains that these form the 'strong containers' to help us live healthy and happy lives.[18] Studies have consistently shown that children with no boundaries are less happy and more anxious than those who grow up with clear rules and expectations. They may well then need to push against these as they grow up, but if they never have them at all they will struggle to flourish.[19]

One of the foremost themes of scripture is God's desire to free people from burdens, whether that is from the burden of captivity, forced labour, oppression or sin.

> 'I relieved your shoulder of the burden;
>   your hands were freed from the basket.'
> v. 6

However, this is not a freedom to do whatever we want, and the Lord provided laws to guide, protect and contain his people. Human beings were always going to fail at keeping the laws and were always going to push against the boundaries set by a loving God, in much the same way that our children are always going to rebel against rules we set them.

Thankfully for us, Jesus took all the burden of human disobedience and rebellion on to himself on the cross, so that, through the grace of God, we can be free and live life in all its fullness. This doesn't mean doing whatever we please, as we will no doubt find that that doesn't lead to a fulfilling life.

The apostle Paul writes that, through Jesus, 'God has done what the law, weakened by the flesh, could not do: by sending his own Son' (Romans 8:3).

Further reading, reflection and prayer

Reading

> 'Come to me, all you that are weary and are carrying heavy burdens, and I will give you rest. Take my yoke upon you, and learn from me, for I am gentle and humble in heart, and you will find rest for your souls. For my yoke is easy, and my burden is light.'
> MATTHEW 11:28–30

Listen

'Sing joyfully' by William Byrd, Clare College Chapel Choir, Timothy Brown, *Tudor Anthems: From the Oxford Book of Tudor Anthems* (1995)

This piece of music is based on Psalm 81:1–4.

Prayer

What thou shalt today provide,
Let me as a child receive;
What tomorrow may betide,
Calmly to thy wisdom leave.
'Tis enough that thou wilt care:
Why should I the burden bear?

John Newton (1725—1807)

183

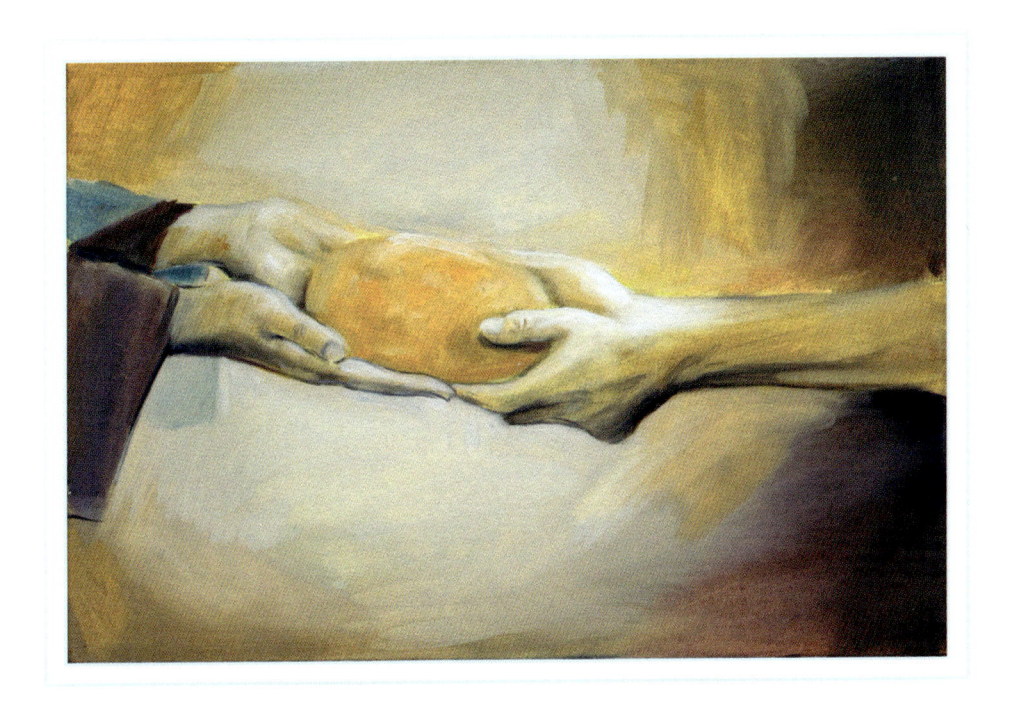

Psalm 82

'Give justice to the weak'

God has taken his place in the divine council;
in the midst of the gods he holds judgement:
'How long will you judge unjustly
   and show partiality to the wicked? *Selah*
Give justice to the weak and the orphan;
   maintain the right of the lowly and the destitute.
Rescue the weak and the needy;
   deliver them from the hand of the wicked.'

They have neither knowledge nor understanding,
   they walk around in darkness;
   all the foundations of the earth are shaken.

I say, 'You are gods,
   children of the Most High, all of you;

> nevertheless, you shall die like mortals,
>> and fall like any prince.'
>
> Rise up, O God, judge the earth,
>> for all the nations belong to you!

My youngest son spent his work experience week with a criminal barrister in Wales and had a most fascinating time seeing the justice system in action. He told me that he watched a case where a man was accused of assaulting three women. He said most people in court believed the women (as he did), but despite this, the man was found not guilty because there wasn't enough evidence to convict 'beyond reasonable doubt'. Compared to many judicial systems across the world, our court system is pretty good, but I can only imagine the pain these three women must have felt, and the pain felt by all people when justice isn't forthcoming. Perhaps, as in the psalm, it feels like 'all the foundations of the earth are shaken' (v. 5).

In this psalm God is imagined as taking his place in the 'divine council', the great court of heaven, and is judging those who have judged unjustly on earth by showing partiality to the wicked (v. 2), not upholding the rights of the poor and the orphans (vv. 2–3), and not saving the weak from exploitation by the strong (v. 4).

At the time the psalm was written, the belief was that the God of Israel was one among many gods, and the psalmist is attempting to show that Israel's God is supreme, with all the others being stupid and incompetent: 'they walk around in darkness' (v. 5). The God of Israel is omniscient and omnipotent but uses this power in a way that is infinitely more just, loving and fair.

One of the parables of Jesus tells of a widow and an unjust judge. She keeps on pleading with him for justice until he eventually gives in and grants it, simply to get rid of her. The parable ends with Jesus saying that God is not like that – 'I tell you, he will quickly grant justice to them' (Luke 18:1–8).

Perhaps this can give us a wider perspective. We are reminded that God is the ultimate judge, the 'one lawgiver and judge who is able to save and to destroy' (James 4:12), and this can release us from having to take on that role ourselves. Our pursuit of justice shouldn't mean we lose focus on those who God cares most about – the voiceless, oppressed, abused and needy.

Further reading, reflection and prayer

Reading

> 'Do not judge, so that you may not be judged. For the judgement you give will be the judgement you get, and the measure you give will be the measure you get. Why do you see the speck in your neighbour's eye but do not notice the log in your own eye?'
> MATTHEW 7:1–3

Listen

'Largo' by Antonio Vivaldi, John C. Williams, *Orquesta Sinfónica de Sevilla, The Seville Concert* (1993)

Prayer

Lord, make me an instrument of your peace.
Where there is hatred, let me sow love;
where there is injury, pardon;
where there is doubt, faith;
where there is despair, hope;
where there is darkness, light;
and where there is sadness, joy.
Attributed to St Francis of Assisi (c. 1181—1226)

189

Psalm 85

'Faithfulness will spring up from the ground'

Lord, you were favourable to your land;
    you restored the fortunes of Jacob.
You forgave the iniquity of your people;
    you pardoned all their sin. *Selah*
You withdrew all your wrath;
    you turned from your hot anger.

Restore us again, O God of our salvation,
    and put away your indignation towards us.
Will you be angry with us forever?
    Will you prolong your anger to all generations?
Will you not revive us again,
    so that your people may rejoice in you?

Show us your steadfast love, O Lord,
    and grant us your salvation.

Let me hear what God the Lord will speak,
    for he will speak peace to his people,
    to his faithful, to those who turn to him in their hearts.
Surely his salvation is at hand for those who fear him,
    that his glory may dwell in our land.

Steadfast love and faithfulness will meet;
    righteousness and peace will kiss each other.
Faithfulness will spring up from the ground,
    and righteousness will look down from the sky.
The Lord will give what is good,
    and our land will yield its increase.
Righteousness will go before him,
    and will make a path for his steps.

I don't get angry very often, but when I do it's normally because someone I love has been hurt or mistreated. I would like to think my anger is always righteous and well deserved, but the last time I remember being really furious was when a close family member left one of my sons in tears by questioning his life choices in a way that I felt undermined him, and us. I massively overreacted and my anger shocked us all, and I had some apologising to do. Thankfully, our family doesn't tend to do the simmering passive anger that can lead to years of division – we're more likely to have a loud, shouty moment, and then kiss and make up.

One of the uncomfortable themes in the Psalms is that of God's anger. It's not something we like to focus on often, and I know I'm much more disposed to consider God's love than his wrath. I think it's a reaction to those spittle-filled preachers by Brixton tube station who shouted at me every time I got back from a hard day's work, exhorting me to repent or face the fires of hell. It never seemed a very effective evangelistic technique. Having said that, the anger of God is an important theme of scripture, and one we can't shy away from.

In the Bible God's anger is generally aroused by three things: people turning away from him; people turning towards idols; people treating other people badly. In much of the Old Testament the understanding was that when bad things happened, such as crops failing or wars being lost, this revealed that God was angry with the people. Conversely when the people turned back to God, then his love would be restored, and this would be shown through the abundance of the land around them; the rains would come, the animals would flourish and food would be plentiful.

The psalmist asks, 'Will you be angry with us forever?' (v. 5), and to answer this question he looks back and remembers that the Lord 'forgave', 'pardoned' and 'turned from your hot anger' (vv. 2–3) in the past, and so surely will do so again. He is remembering the restoration after the Babylonian exile, when the Israelites were able to return to Jerusalem, rebuild the temple and restore their community life.

The imagery in this psalm of restoration is profoundly beautiful. It embodies the characteristics of reconciling love as if they are two people meeting and embracing on a country road:

> Steadfast love and faithfulness will meet;
> > righteousness and peace will kiss each other.
> v. 10

'Faithfulness will spring up from the ground', and all that is right with the world will 'look down from the sky' (v. 11). This psalm contains a wonderful image of shalom, which the bishop of Oxford describes as 'one of the deepest, richest, broadest words in the whole of the Bible… shorthand for the whole vision of the kingdom of God: a world where God's will is done on earth as in heaven'.[20]

After any conflict, whether a breakdown in relationship or an all-out war, meaningful restoration will only come if both sides move towards one another. My argument with my family member needed us both to recognise our mistakes and apologise to each other. This isn't always possible in this life, and sadly some conflicts seem to be intractable this side of heaven.

We are, however, invited to nurture the green shoots of shalom in whatever ways we can, because in doing so we are part of the restoration work of the kingdom.

Further reading, reflection and prayer

Reading

> Be angry but do not sin; do not let the sun go down on your anger, and do not make room for the devil.
> EPHESIANS 4:26–27

Listen

'Psalm 85: A psalm of lament' by Poor Bishop Hooper (2021)

This piece is part of a project called 'EveryPsalm'.

Prayer

O God, from whom to be turned is to fall,
to whom to be turned is to rise,
and in whom to stand is to abide forever;
grant us in all our duties thy help,
in all our perplexities thy guidance,
in all our dangers thy protection,
and in all our sorrows thy peace.

Augustine of Hippo (354–430)

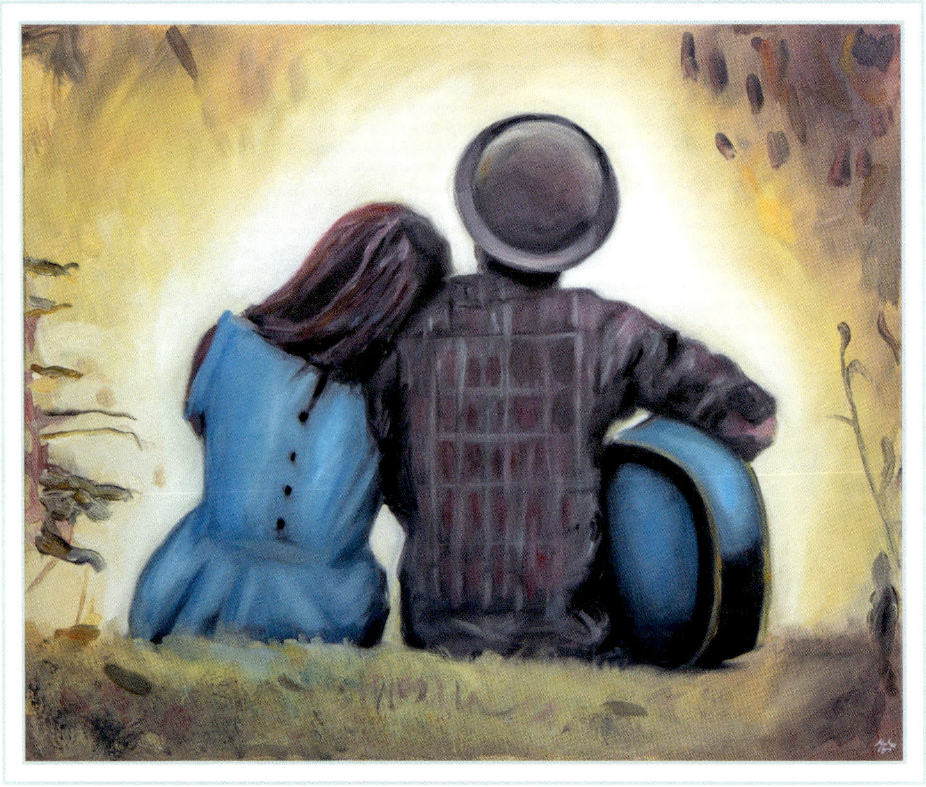

Psalm 87

'All my springs are in you'

On the holy mount stands the city he founded;
  the Lord loves the gates of Zion
  more than all the dwellings of Jacob.
Glorious things are spoken of you,
  O city of God. *Selah*

Among those who know me I mention Rahab and Babylon;
  Philistia, too, and Tyre, with Cush –
  'This one was born there,' they say.

And of Zion it shall be said,
  'This one and that one were born in it,'
  for the Most High himself will establish it.

> The Lord records, as he registers the peoples,
> 'This one was born there.' *Selah*
>
> Singers and dancers alike say,
> 'All my springs are in you.'

In his profound book *Falling Upwards*, Richard Rohr writes about the spirituality of the two halves of life. He contends that the main tasks of the first half of life are about building up our resources and identity, working out what makes us significant and finding those people who will accompany us on the journey. These are all good and necessary containers for the deeper journey of the second half of life, which, he argues, is discovering 'the task within the task', which involves descent, failure, letting go, inevitable suffering, growth and freedom. Our problem, and the problem for most of western culture, is that we feel so comfortable in the shallows of the first half that we don't want to set out into the deeper waters of the second. He writes:

> Setting out is always a leap of faith, a risk in the deepest sense of the term, and yet an adventure too. The familiar and the habitual are so falsely reassuring, and most of us make our homes there permanently.[21]

This journey of 'falling upwards', as Rohr describes it, is experienced throughout scripture and particularly in the psalms. Israel reached the peak of political importance at the time of David and Solomon, and the magnificent temple in Jerusalem (as described in 1 Kings 6) was a vivid, visual reminder of this. However, when we consider the stories of scripture where the deepest learning happened, these were never at times of plenty, when the temple was intact, the community was prosperous and the kings were winning wars.

The stories we cling on to are the ones about how God led the people in the wilderness when they didn't know where their next meal was coming from (Exodus 16); or the ones about the small boy facing up to a giant of an enemy with only five smooth stones (1 Samuel 17); or the story of the prophet Elisha who had almost given up hope until he met a woman who had also reached the end of her tether but offered him her final drop of oil, which made all the difference in the world to both of them (2 Kings 4:1–7).

This psalm speaks of a holy place, a mount where a city is founded and where all are counted in and welcomed – 'This one was born there' (vv. 4, 6). It is interesting that all the places mentioned were all natural enemies of Israel, so not 'born there' in a literal sense: Rahab is another term for Egypt; Babylon was the great oppressor to the north who destroyed the first temple; Philistia was Judah's traditional foe.

The psalm reminds us that God longs to welcome all people into his presence – we all belong there, and the good news is that we don't have to strive hard to achieve it. From starting with an image of a gated city on a mountain, the psalm ends with a totally different metaphor for faith, that of a fresh spring welling up from within, to bring joy, song and dance: 'Singers and dancers alike say, "All my springs are in you"' (v. 7). This seems to me to be a very 'second half of life' image.

Further reading, reflection and prayer

Reading

> Jesus said to her, 'Everyone who drinks of this water will be thirsty again, but those who drink of the water that I will give them will never be thirsty. The water that I will give will become in them a spring of water gushing up to eternal life.'
> JOHN 4:13–14

Listen

The words of this Taizé song come from this prayer attributed to Teresa of Ávila.

'Nada te Turbe' by Taizé Community, *Laudate Omnes Gentes* (2002)

Prayer

Let nothing disturb you,
Nothing dismay you;
All things are passing:
God never changes.
Patient endurance
Attains all it strives for:
Those who have God
Find they lack nothing.
God alone suffices.
St Teresa of Ávila (1515–82)

202

Psalm 131

'I am like a weaned child with its mother'

My heart is not proud, Lord,
   my eyes are not haughty;
I do not concern myself with great matters
   or things too wonderful for me.
But I have calmed and quietened myself,
   I am like a weaned child with its mother;
   like a weaned child I am content.

Israel, put your hope in the Lord
   both now and forevermore.
(NIV)

Darren has been coming to the same retreat house in Oxfordshire three times a year for 30 years. I met him over a meal while on retreat and asked him what drew him back time and time again. He told me, 'As soon as I arrive it feels like I'm safe again – at home.' Darren lives with multiple disabilities and sensory issues which make his life hard and a struggle in many ways. He said that once he stepped over the threshold of the centre he felt as if he was 'enveloped in a warm embrace', and that each time he came he went away with the strength to carry on.

I've been going on retreat for many years and understand what Darren means by this. As an extrovert I often surround myself with people and projects and am never happier than ticking off a 'to-do' list feeling proud of all I've achieved. This can be exhausting, and I know that I need to take myself away every so often to recharge my spiritual batteries and remind myself that my value is not in what I do or whom I impress. I often find it takes me a few days to learn to relax into the solitude and feel comfortable with silence, but once I do I feel at home in myself again. It can be a huge relief to realise that if I achieved absolutely nothing at all, I would still be loved by God. It's actually a very hard lesson to learn.

This is one of the 15 'song of ascents' (Psalms 120—134), which most scholars believe were songs sung by worshippers as they travelled to Jerusalem to attend the three major Jewish festivals of Passover, Shavuot and Sukkot. At only three verses it is one of the shortest psalms (117 is the shortest with only two verses), but brief though it may be, it contains an important message.

There is a beautiful simplicity to it – no petitions are made, no problems are voiced, nothing is expected or asked for. There is a sense that, for this moment, all that is needed is to be still, to be quiet and to trust. The image of the 'weaned child with its mother' is a poignant one and makes us think of the deep, satisfied sleep of a child lying in its mother's arms. The child is weaned, which means it is no longer breastfeeding and so the contentment doesn't come from having been given breastmilk, but from the knowledge that they are safe and loved. The child might have been crying just moments before, but now doesn't need anything else, and simply lies quietly contented in the warm embrace of its mother.

The image of God as a mother hugging her child might be a surprising one, but it's not unusual in scripture: in Hosea God is described as a mother bear protecting her young (Hosea 13:8); in Isaiah God is both a comforting mother and a woman in labour (Isaiah 66:13; 42:14); and Jesus described himself as a mother hen gathering her brood (Matthew 23:37; Luke 13:34).

The psalm ends with a plea for Israel to 'hope in the Lord', and there is a sense of waiting and hoping that permeates this psalm and the ones that precede and follow it. They are waiting for the Messiah, the one who would bring about salvation, peace and true contentment. Christians believe that this waiting came to fruition in the person of Jesus Christ, 'God made flesh', who entered our world as a vulnerable baby, reliant on the love and care of his own mother, Mary.

It may be that we are struggling with any number of 'great matters' that are 'too wonderful' or too confusing, painful or exhausting for us to bear. Perhaps we too, like Darren, are invited to enter a time of solitude for a while, whether this is on a few days' retreat or just half an hour of silence in a chair at home. At times all we can do is to be quiet and still ourselves, resting in the loving embrace of God, who is both mother and father to us and who calls us home into her/his presence.

Further reading, reflection and prayer

Reading

> In the morning, while it was still very dark, [Jesus] got up and went out to a deserted place, and there he prayed.
> MARK 1:35

Listen

This song is a conversation between someone trying hard to prove their worth and God's response to them.

'Dear God' by Cory Asbury, *To Love a Fool* (2020)

Prayer

Almighty God, in whom we live and move and have our being,
thou hast made us for thyself, and our hearts are restless until they find their rest in thee;
grant us such purity of heart and strength of purpose,
that no selfish passion may hinder us from knowing thy will,
and no weakness from doing it;
but that in thy light we may see light,
and in thy service find perfect freedom,
through Jesus Christ our Lord. Amen.

Augustine of Hippo (354–430)

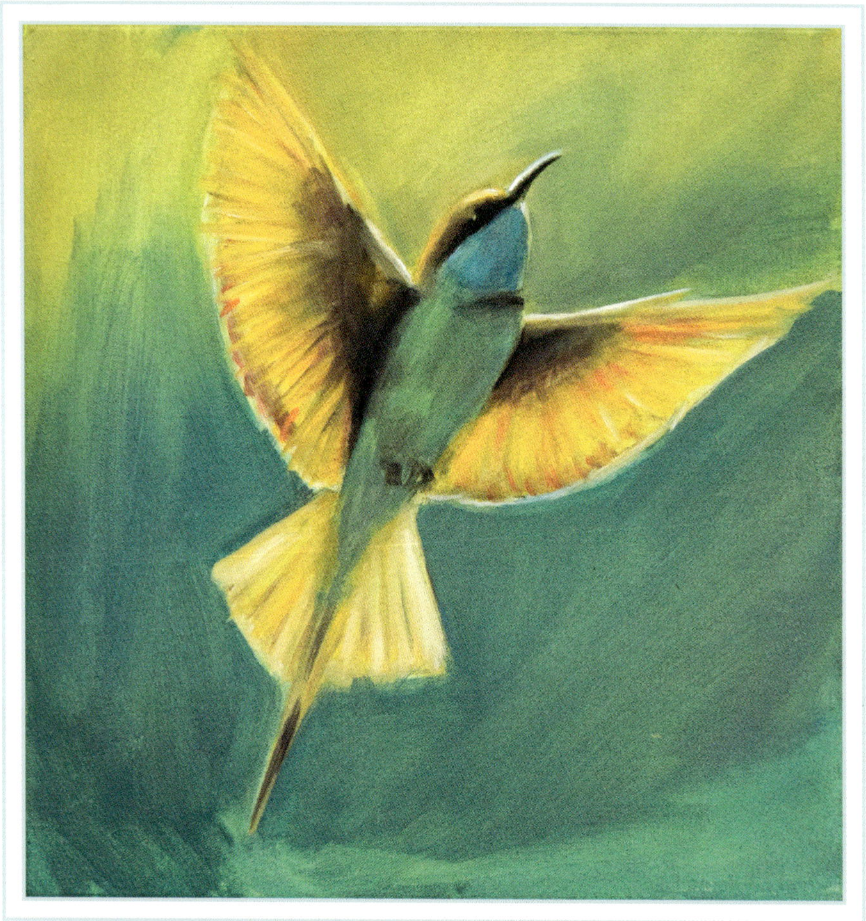

Psalm 139

'If I take the wings of the morning… even there your hand shall lead me'

O Lord, you have searched me and known me.
   You know when I sit down and when I rise up;
you discern my thoughts from far away.
You search out my path and my lying down
   and are acquainted with all my ways.
Even before a word is on my tongue,
   O Lord, you know it completely…
   Such knowledge is too wonderful for me;
   it is so high that I cannot attain it.

Where can I go from your spirit?
   Or where can I flee from your presence?
If I ascend to heaven, you are there;

> if I make my bed in Sheol, you are there.
> If I take the wings of the morning
> > and settle at the farthest limits of the sea,
> even there your hand shall lead me,
> > and your right hand shall hold me fast.
> If I say, 'Surely the darkness shall cover me,
> > and night wraps itself around me',
> even the darkness is not dark to you;
> > the night is as bright as the day,
> > for darkness is as light to you.
>
> For it was you who formed my inward parts;
> > you knit me together in my mother's womb.
> I praise you, for I am fearfully and wonderfully made.
> > Wonderful are your works;
> > that I know very well…
>
> Search me, O God, and know my heart;
> > test me and know my thoughts.
> See if there is any wicked way in me,
> > and lead me in the way everlasting.
>
> vv. 1–4, 6–14, 23–24

There is something wonderful about observing the creative process – seeing a painting emerging on a blank piece of paper, hearing a piece of newly composed music or reading an imaginative story. I love watching Micah when he's hard at work painting. Once he has an idea in his mind, he spends every waking hour focused on it. He doesn't seem to get tired and keeps going until he somehow knows when it's finished, and it's only then that he's satisfied.

This psalm is a song of praise to God the creator from someone who is utterly awestruck to think that not only have they been 'fearfully and wonderfully made' (v. 14), but also that their creator knows everything about them, cares about every detail of their life and will continue to be present throughout it.

The thought that there is nowhere they can go to get away from God's love – whether they 'take the wings of the morning' (v. 9), plumb the darkest depths or even enter the realm of death (Sheol) – overwhelms the psalmist: 'Such knowledge is too wonderful for me; it is so high that I cannot attain it' (v. 6). For some, the idea of being fully known (v. 1) by God and hemmed in 'behind and before' (v. 5) is an alarming prospect. Does God really know everything about us? Is there really nowhere we can go that is outside of God's omnipresent gaze? This might make us feel uncomfortable and afraid, or secure and comforted, depending on our view of God.

Charles Spurgeon, one of the foremost Baptist preachers of the 19th century, preached on this psalm and spoke of God as a 'best friend' who never leaves us, and whose 'great observant eye of divine love is never closed'. This is a frightening prospect if we think of God as rather like an unforgiving tyrant or a disapproving parent.

In this psalm we are invited to reflect on God as the loving creator who takes care over each creation he has made. Spurgeon calls his listeners to look to Jesus, who was 'in very nature God', and so reveals to us what God the Father is like:

> I wish that all of you knew this blessed experience of which I have been speaking. Some of you do not. You are afraid of God, you are afraid of His seeing you, you are afraid to go to Him. See, then, here is Jesus Christ who took upon Him our nature though He also is God. Go to Him, trust Him, believe in Him, then He will make you to be a child of God and you will not be afraid of your Father.[22]

Amen!

Further reading, reflection and prayer

Reading

Let the same mind be in you that was in Christ Jesus,
who, though he was in the form of God,
    did not regard equality with God
    as something to be exploited,
but emptied himself,
    taking the form of a slave,
    being born in human likeness.
And being found in appearane as a human,
    he humbled himself
    and became obedient to the point of death –
    even death on a cross.
PHILIPPIANS 2:5–8

Listen

'Peace (arr. A. Frey for euphonium and orchestra)' by John Golland, Adam Frey, New Zealand Symphony Orchestra, Bruce Hangen, *Majestic Journey* (2007)

Prayer

O Lord, who has mercy on all, take away from me my sins, and mercifully kindle in me the fire of your Holy Spirit. Take away from me the heart of stone, and give me the heart of flesh, a heart to love and adore you, a heart to delight in you, to follow you and to enjoy you, for Christ's sake.

Ambrose of Milan (c. 339–397)

Notes

1 Athanasius, *On the Incarnation,* cited in Gordon Wenham, *The Psalter Reclaimed: Praying and praising the Psalms* (Crossway, 2013), p. 15.

2 **chch.ox.ac.uk/news/christ-church-cathedral-unveils-first-new-stained-glass-130-years**

3 Thomas Aquinas, *Sermons on the Two Precepts of Charity and the Ten Precepts of the Law* (1273), cited by Richard Rohr, **cac.org/daily-meditations/the-first-bible-2019-02-20**

4 **saveourwildisles.org.uk**

5 Margaret Atwood on storytelling as a tool of tyrnats', The Story, 20 October 2023, **thestory.au/articles/margaret-atwood-interview-storytelling-as-a-tool-of-tyrants**

6 Walter Brueggemann, *Spirituality of the Psalms* (Augsberg Fortress, 2001), p. 25.

7 John Wesley's 'Directions for singing' was included as an appendage to *Select Hymns: with Tunes Annext* (1761)

8 You can learn more about the daily Examen at **ignatianspirituality.com/ignatian-prayer/the-examen**

9 I recommend this website for routes in the UK: **britishpilgrimage.org**

10 Megan Daffern, *Songs of the Spirit: A psalm a day for Lent and Easter* (SPCK, 2017), p. 4.

11 Mother Teresa, *Come Be My Light: The revealing private writings of the Saint of Calcutta*, edited by Brian Kolodiejchuk (Doubleday, 2007), pp. 192–93.

12 Cited in C.H. Spurgeon, *The Treasury of David*, Vol. 1 (Marshall Brothers, 1869), p. 14, available at: **classicchristianlibrary.com/ot_section2.html**

13 Brené Brown, *The Gifts of Imperfection* (Hazleden Publishing, 2018), pp. 12–14.

14 Stephen Cave, *Immortality: The quest to live forever and how it drives civilization* (Biteback, 2012), p. 16.

15 **poetryfoundation.org/poems/46565/Ozymandias**

16 'Evidence Review: Loneliness in Later Life' (June 2015), available at: **ageuk.org.uk/our-impact/policy-research/publications/reports-and-briefings**

17 **annachaplaincy.org.uk**

18 Richard Rohr, *Falling Upward: A spirituality of for the two halves of life* (revised edition, John Wiley and Sons, 2024), p. 127.

19 Jonathan Haidt, *The Anxious Generation: How the great rewiring of childhood is causing an epidemic of mental illness* (Allen Lane, 2024). This book is a stark wakeup call to the dangers of unregulated social media on the psychological well-being of children and young people.

20 From a sermon given by the bishop of Oxford at St Edberg's Church, Bicester on 5 November 2023, **blogs.oxford.anglican.org/blessed-are-the-peacemakers**

21 Rohr, Falling Upward, p. 24.

22 C.H. Spurgeon, 'Our thoughts about God's thoughts', sermon no. 2609, 1 November 1883, **spurgeongems.org/sermon/chs2609.pdf**

Space for reflection

GARDEN SONG

SPACE FOR REFLECTION 219

220 GARDEN SONG

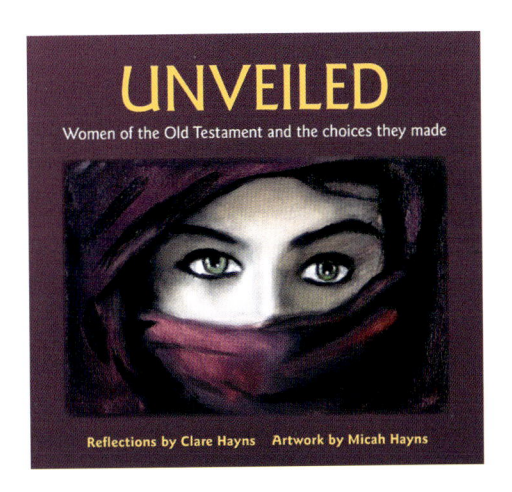

Some women of the Hebrew scriptures are well known, but many others are barely remembered. Even when they are, we often don't pause on them long enough to think about what we might learn from them. *Unveiled*, written with frankness and humour and illustrated with striking artwork from a young Oxford-based artist, explores the stories of 40 women in 40 days. Each reflection ends with a short application to everyday life, guidance for further thought and a prayer.

Unveiled
Women of the Old Testament and the choices they made
Reflections by Clare Hayns and artwork by Micah Hayns
978 1 80039 072 0 £14.99

brfonline.org.uk

A 40-day journey exploring the themes of hope and new life through vivd biblical images, *Holding Onto Hope* can be used through Lent or during nay 40-day period. We start with how all creation praises God and then explore the agricultural pattern of sowing, growing and harvesting before moving to the gracious promises and invitations God makes to his people. Next come images of God as our help and refuge. Finally, we focus on our new life in Christ.

Holding Onto Hope
40 days of God's encouragement through art and reflections
Amy Boucher Pye and Leo Boucher
978 1 80039 200 7 £12.99

brfonline.org.uk

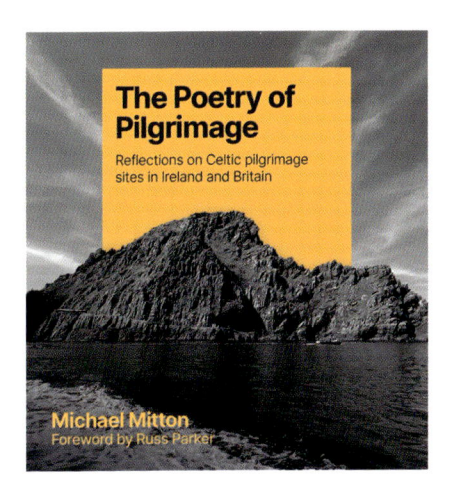

Drawing from his experience of co-leading pilgrimages in Britain and Ireland, Michael Mitton captures the essence of 23 significant pilgrimage sites for anyone from experienced pilgrims to armchair pilgrims. Each chapter outlines the story of the Celtic saint who founded the site, together with information about the location, a poem inspired by the author's experience of that place, a reflective question, a suggested Bible reading and a photo of the site.

Poetry of Pilgrimage
Reflections on Celtic pilgrimage sites in Ireland and Britain
Michael Mitton
978 1 80039 321 9 £12.99

brfonline.org.uk

BRF Ministries

Inspiring people of all ages to grow in Christian faith

BRF Ministries is the home of Anna Chaplaincy, Living Faith, Messy Church and Parenting for Faith

As a charity, our work would not be possible without fundraising and gifts in wills. To find out more and to donate, visit brf.org.uk/give or call +44 (0)1235 462305

Registered with FUNDRAISING REGULATOR